Silly Songs, Surprising Stories, and Supreme Court Justices

The Wild Fun-tier of Stone-Campbell Movement History

John Young

Silly Songs, Surprising Stories, and Supreme Court Justices: The Wild Fun-tier of Stone-Campbell Movement History

Published by Heritage Christian University Press

Copyright © 2025 by John Young

Manufactured in the United States of America

Cataloging-in-Publication Data

John Young, 1989–

Silly songs, surprising stories, and Supreme Court Justices: the wild fun-tier of Stone-Campbell Movement history / by John Young

p. cm.

ISBN 978-1-956811-99-5 (pbk.); 979-8-89733-000-3 (e-book)

1. Restoration movement (Christianity). 2. Christian Church (Disciples of Christ). 3. Christian biography. I. Author. II. Title.

BX7077 .Y68 2021 286.609—dc20

Library of Congress Control Number: 2025931514

Cover design by Brad McKinnon and Brittany VanderMaas

For more information:

Heritage Christian University Press

PO Box HCU

3625 Helton Drive

Florence, AL 35630

www.hcu.edu/publications

Praise for John Young

Young skillfully chases down some intriguing rumors and rabbits involving members of the Stone-Campbell Movement and their connections to the broader American social and political landscape, including some high-profile figures. He writes with just enough depth to keep these vignettes engaging, yet accessible. Anyone with at least a casual interest in Restoration and American history—and a mild sense of humor—will find this book an enjoyable read.

— Calvin Cockrell, Media Editor, *Christian Chronicle*

Dr. Young masterfully weaves the arts of story-telling and historical research to explore the Restoration Movement's unknown recesses. He takes on little known facts, legends, and rumors to provide the reader with what really happened in a colorful and personal way.

— Dr. Laws Rushing II, Mars Hill Bible School President

John Young's latest book is a special volume of "interesting" stories, taking you through surprisingly suspenseful and fascinating yet forgotten events within the Stone-Campbell Movement. Whether you're a history buff or just curious about the historical impact of this significant religious group, this collection of stories will leave you with a wealth of information and a newfound interest in this American movement and its "truly global impact."

— Zack Martin, Instructor of Historical Theology and Dean of Students, Heritage Christian University

To Candace and Nathan.
You two are, now and forever, my sources of true joy.

Contents

Acknowledgments

Any book-length history project—even one as subject to the whims of its author's peculiar interests and sense of humor as this one—is a collective endeavor, and it is important that the person whose name is on the front cover share the credit and/or blame as is due.

In writing the blog posts, conference papers, and random musings that comprise this collection, I accumulated debts to the libraries of several institutions, including Amridge University, Heritage Christian University, and Sherrod Avenue Church of Christ.

I am also indebted to readers of my now-abandoned blogs and to the gracious audience members for the assortment of papers I gave at the Conference on Faith and History, the Southern Studies Conference, the Stone-Campbell Journal Conference, and a handful of one-off events.

I am appreciative of my fellow faculty members, staff, and administrators of the schools where I teach for the different kinds of support and encouragement they gave me along the way.

Finally, I am eternally grateful to Candace, Nathan, my parents, and the rest of you who make my life rich, meaningful, and rewarding.

Towards a Truly Global History: Introduction

In 2014, the editors of *The Stone-Campbell Movement: A Global History* set for themselves the lofty goal of "explor[ing] not only the Movement's North American streams, but its significant global development ... ."[1] It is my opinion that by and large, they succeeded in the task. The team of historians, representing various movement fellowships and historical methods, offered up a textbook-like survey that covered over two centuries' worth of developments on six of the seven continents.

But what of the seventh? Can a history truly be "global" if it overlooks our planet's coldest and southernmost continent? I ask these questions tongue in cheek, mostly, but having long had an interest in the history of the human exploration of Antarctica, I wondered if the Stone-Campbell Movement might have had some sort of impact on that story. Perhaps because of the continent's vanishingly small

---

1. D. Newell Williams, Douglas A. Foster, and Paul M. Blowers, eds., *The Stone-Campbell Movement: A Global History* (St. Louis, MO: Chalice Press, 2013), vii.

human population, ranging only in the low thousands and composed almost entirely of scientists and support staff, little has been written about religious faith and practice "on the ice."[2]

McMurdo Station

Memoirs of Antarctic stays occasionally make reference to religiosity (or irreligiosity), as is the case in Nicholas Johnson's *Big Dead Place*, which observes that

> Identification with one's door decorations in McMurdo [Station] increases with abundance or with particularly obsessive themes, such as top to bottom Christmas decorations, or more than ten Peanuts cartoons, or more than one cross or other unmistakable Christian symbol, at which point one might be referred to as 'the Snoopy freak' or 'the Jesus guy.'[3]

The most extensive scholarly treatment of which I am aware is Ellen C. Frye's essay "The Ant-architecture of Religion and Spirituality in Antarctica," which touches on

---

2. One exception is a creative work by Eric G. Wilson, titled *The Spiritual History of Ice: Romanticism, Science, and the Imagination* (New York: Palgrave Macmillan, 2003).

3. Nicholas Johnson, *Big Dead Place: Inside the Strange and Menacing World of Antarctica* (Los Angeles: Feral House, 2005), 20.

the religious lives of a few Antarctic notables and intro-
duces the eight dedicated places of worship on the
continent.

Chapel of the Snows

Of these eight, the nondenominational Chapel of the
Snows, located at the US-affiliated McMurdo Station, is the
most likely to have some sort of Stone-Campbell connection. It seems almost certain to me that members of the
Stone-Campbell fellowships have made their way through
McMurdo given its status as the largest (by a wide margin)
community on the continent. Yet, I have been unable to find
any direct evidence as such.

Does that mean that we are kept from a truly global
history? Not yet. Later in the book, I will introduce some of
the most important American politicians and jurists associated with the movement, but I will give a slight spoiler here
by telling you that Ronald Reagan grew up in the Disciples
of Christ and even attended the Disciples-affiliated Eureka
College. As president, Reagan had several opportunities to
shape—and reshape—America's Antarctic policy. Just over a
year into his first term, for instance, he released a presidential memorandum which put forth the following guidance:

- *The United States Antarctic Program shall be maintained at a level providing an active and influential presence in Antarctica designed to support the range of U.S. Antarctic interests.*
- *This presence shall include the conduct of scientific activities in major disciplines; year-round occupation of the South Pole and two coastal stations; and availability of related necessary logistics support.*
- *Every effort shall be made to manage the program in a manner that maximizes cost effectiveness and return on investment.*[4]

In late 1984, Reagan had another opportunity to give his support to Antarctic interests when, just after his successful reelection campaign, he sent a message to the scientists and others living on the US bases to thank them for twenty-five years of successful work following the adoption of the Antarctic Treaty. According to Reagan, the

> work in Antarctica continues to reflect the universal ideals reflected in the Treaty. I commend your commitment to the search for knowledge and send my best wishes to all of you for a productive season.[5]

---

4. "President's Memorandum Regarding Antarctica," February 5, 1982, https://www.nsf.gov/geo/opp/ant/memo_6646.jsp. For some additional context, see Ronald W. Scott, "Protecting United States Interests in Antarctica," *San Diego Law Review* 26 (1989): 575–623, especially pages 602–603, 609, and 613.

5. "Message on the 25th Anniversary of the Antarctic Treaty," November 26, 1984, https://www.reaganlibrary.gov/archives/speech/message-25th-anniversary-antarctic-treaty.

And in the spring of 1988, the US joined the *Montreal Protocol on Substances that Deplete the Ozone Layer*, a pact with enormous environmental implications for Antarctica, with Reagan describing himself as "pleased to sign the instrument of ratification... an extremely important environmental agreement."[6]

It is this kind of unusual, unexpected, and off-the-beaten-path story to which this volume is devoted. The stories and studies included in this book, along with a handful of journal articles that have been published elsewhere,[7] have been researched and written primarily or exclusively because I thought they were interesting rabbits to chase. A few have been given a trial run in blog or conference paper form, but for the most part, this is new material indicative of how I've spent my writing time over the last two or three years. And while there is no overarching thesis driving the book, I have tried to arrange the chapters into a somewhat logical itinerary with a point of connection from one topic to the next.

Compared to my previous solo-author books, this volume is probably less spiritually encouraging than *Visions of Restoration* and perhaps less scholarly in its tone than

---

6. "Statement on Signing the Montreal Protocol on Ozone-Depleting Substances," April 5, 1988, https://www.reaganlibrary.gov/archives/speech/statement-signing-montreal-protocol-ozone-depleting-substances. For more context, see James McClintock, *Lost Antarctica: Adventures in a Disappearing Land* (New York: St. Martin's Griffin, 2012), 212.

7. These include "Disciples of Christ and The University of Alabama School of Religion That Wasn't," *Alabama Review* 75. 3 (July 2022): 199–224; "Longing for a Better Country: The Stone-Campbell Movement and the Search for Atlantis," *Journal of Discipliana* 75.1 (2022); and "The House of 'Mirrors': A Historical-Statistical Analysis of Five Lectureships Associated with Churches of Christ-Affiliated Schools, 1920–2020," *Restoration Quarterly* 65.3 (2023): 171–179.

Redrawing the Blueprints.[8] But I hope it is spiritually encouraging in some measure, and I know that I have relied heavily on my academic training as a historian in bringing this project to fruition. Above all, though, I hope that this book is *interesting*—that it reminds us that history can also be fun and maybe even a little bit silly.

---

8. *Visions of Restoration: The History of Churches of Christ* (Florence, AL: Cypress Publications, 2019); *Redrawing the Blueprints for the Early Church: Historical Ecclesiology in and around the Stone-Campbell Movement* (Florence, AL: Heritage Christian University Press, 2021).

Chapter 1

Our Man in Havana

Juan Antonio Monroy, Fidel Castro, and the Churches of Christ in Cuba

AT THE VERY beginning of 1911—the first of January, at seven o'clock in the morning, to be exact—the noted Churches of Christ minister T.B. Larimore and his fiancée, Emma Page, got married and set out together for a year-long evangelistic trip. (How's that for a honeymoon?) The newly-weds' journeys would take them "From Maine to Mexico, From Canada to Cuba," as the subtitle of Emma Page's travelogue reflects, and most of their stops included preaching stints from T.B.[1] Yet at Havana, Cuba, their final port of call before returning home, the Larimores were on vacation. For a week in early December, the couple explored the city and the surrounding area, taking in its art, architecture, and activism. The only church building they visited was the Columbus Cathedral, and their only connection to the Churches of Christ or the broader Stone-Campbell Move-

---

1. Emma Page Larimore, *Life, Letters, and Sermons of T.B. Larimore* (Nashville, TN: Gospel Advocate, 1931), 20; Emma Page Larimore, *Our Corner Book: From Maine to Mexico, From Canada to Cuba* (Nashville, TN: Publishing House of the M.E. Church, South, 1912), 14.

ment came from a chance encounter with one Esther
Wilson, who worked at a tourist information booth and who
had met T.B. Larimore previously in Florida.[2]

This seeming disinterest in more firmly establishing the
Stone-Campbell religious heritage on the island was part of
a broader trend. An early effort begun by the Disciples of
Christ in 1899 ended twenty years later when the denomination traded its Cuban congregations to the Presbyterians
in exchange for a similar number of churches in Puerto
Rico.[3] Congregations established by the Churches of Christ
proved more numerous and more durable, perhaps due to
the prominence of some of the preachers who championed
the work. J.D. Tant, for instance, proposed the establishment of a Christian (by which he meant Churches of
Christ-affiliated) colony in Cuba. A.B. Lipscomb, a close
relative   of   the   namesake   of   David

---

2.   Larimore, *Our Corner Book*, 187–188.

3.   D. Newell Williams, Douglas A. Foster, and Paul M. Blowers, eds.,
The Stone-Campbell Movement: A Global History (St. Louis, MO: Chalice
Press, 2013), 146–147; William J. Nottingham and William J. Morgan,
"Latin America and the Caribbean, Missions in, 1. Christian Church (Dis-
ciples of Christ)," in Douglas A. Foster et al, eds., *Encyclopedia of the
Stone-Campbell Movement* (Grand Rapids, MI: Eerdmans, 2004), 457;
Carmelo Alvarez, "The Stone-Campbell Movement in Latin America and
the Caribbean," *Leaven* 17.3 (2009): 125. As the authors of *A History of
Churches of Christ in Cuba* note, "since this was before the split, the argument could be made that these missionaries represented what are known
today as Churches of Christ .... However, these missionaries were sent by
the Foreign Christian Missionary Service (FCMS), which remained affili-
ated with the Disciples of Christ; it's best to see these early works as being
of the Disciples." See Jose Antonio Fernandez and Timothy Archer, *A
History of Churches of Christ in Cuba* (Abilene, TX: Herald of Truth
Publications, 2015), 13.

Lipscomb University, likewise called attention to the need for evangelistic efforts there.[4]

This last push belatedly led, over two decades after the Larimores' trip, to successful church plantings under the leadership of Tampa-area ministers Ernesto Estevez and Jose Ricardo Jiminez. By the late 1950s, congregations of the Churches of Christ in Cuba numbered 161, with a total membership of around five thousand. An evangelistic radio broadcast sent out from Havana helped pave the way for this rapid expansion.[5] Estevez even had a moment of meaningful political influence when he developed a cost-saving plan for Cuban farmers; the proposal received approval from the Cuban president, Carlos Prio Socarras, and was scheduled to be unveiled publicly during his next presidential address.[6]

4. Earl Irvin West, *The Search for the Ancient Order*, vol. 4 (Germantown, TN: Religious Book Service, 1987), 394–395.

5. Williams, Foster, and Blowers, eds., *Global History*, 297.

6. West, *Search for the Ancient Order*, vol. 4, 398.

Carlos Prio Sacarras

However, strongman and former president Fulgencio Batista staged a coup against Socarras in 1952.

Fulgencio Batista

His seizure of power brought, along with the end of democratic rule, significant criticism, including, of course, from Fidel Castro, who first tried to overthrow Batista in 1953 and then succeeded in the task in 1959.[7]

Fidel Castro

Political turmoil, state hostility to organized religion, and the difficulty of getting resources from the outside world led to a sharp numerical decline among the Churches of Christ—from 161 congregations down to fifteen, and from approximately five thousand members down to under four hundred, by the late 1980s.[8] Writing about the Christian faith more broadly, Derek Cooper summarizes in *Introduction to World Christian History* that

7. Lawrence A. Clayton and Michael L. Conniff, *A History of Modern Latin America*, 2nd ed. (Belmont, CA: Thomson Wadsworth, 2005), 440.

8. Williams, Foster, and Blowers, eds., *Global History*, 297. Slightly different numbers are given in Tim Archer, "What Can't Be Embargoed: US-Cuban Church Relations," *Missio Dei Journal* 14 (2023), https://missiodeijournal.com/issues/md-14/authors/md-14-archer, but the overall trajectory remains the same.

The consequences of the revolution—though most Cubans enjoyed freedom from the former dictator Fulgencio Batista—have resulted in impoverishment for not only the people in general but also the church. Many of the Catholic and Protestant clergy—as well as the elites of society—fled the island after Castro took control. Before Castro's revolution, in fact, Protestant missions had made great progress on the island after Cuba gained its independence from Spain in 1898. It was actually so successful that, at the time of the revolution, Cuba contained "one of the largest Protestant populations and most indigenized Protestant Church establishments of any country in Latin America."[9]

However, a chance meeting between the Churches of Christ evangelist and journalist Juan Antonio Monroy and Fidel Castro—a brief exchange that took place at the inauguration of Nicaraguan president Daniel Ortega in 1979—led to Monroy receiving a visa and eventually making dozens of evangelistic trips to Cuba. Through these and related labors, Monroy helped bring financial and physical support to the handful of remaining congregations who had long been cut off from their coreligionists. "In cooperation with Cuban workers," the authors of *The Stone-Campbell Movement: A Global History* note, "these efforts resulted in one hundred twenty congregations with a membership of

---

9. Derek Cooper, *Introduction to World Christian History* (Downers Grove, IL: IVP Academic, 2016), 158–159. For an interesting cross-tradition comparison between Churches of Christ and the Southern Baptist Convention, see Colton Babbitt, "Caudill Under El Caudillo: Southern Baptists, Cuba, and the Origins of Conservatism, 1959–1979 (MA thesis, Florida Atlantic University, 2019).

almost five thousand by 2009."[10] So, who was Juan Antonio Monroy, and how did this indefatigable evangelist take advantage of an unusually open door?

Monroy, born in Rabat, Morocco, on June 13, 1929, was the product of a brief marriage between a French Marxist father and Spanish Catholic mother. "I grew up between Karl Marx and the Vatican," he later reflected, "although atheism appealed to me more than religion."[11] Monroy eventually came to faith in 1950, however, a few years after his family had relocated to Tangier. Attending a religious service out of boredom one rainy day, he heard the preaching of a Cuban minister, Ruben Lores, whose wife Dana was the daughter of an elder from the Disciples of Christ. Though this gave Monroy an indirect connection to the Stone-Campbell Movement, it would take nearly a decade and a half for him to land in the Churches of Christ specifically. Part of that fourteen-year period was spent in Franco's army, which Monroy, a Spanish citizen, had joined with the hopes of traveling and evangelizing. (Perhaps unsurprisingly, Monroy's outspoken faith instead led to harassment from the decidedly Catholic religious establishment.)[12]

Aside from his time in the armed forces, Monroy stayed busy during these decades, primarily as an outspoken proponent of religious freedom. He wrote a book spotlighting the persecution of Spanish Protestants which received considerable attention; one of his readers was the British lawyer and human rights activist Peter Benenson,

---

10. Williams, Foster, and Blowers, eds., *Global History*, 298.
11. Juan Antonio Monroy, *An Autobiography*, trans. Carolina Tolosa Archer (Abilene, TX: ACU Press, 2011), 12.
12. Monroy, *An Autobiography*, 11–33.

who invited Monroy to speak at the inaugural meeting of what is known today as Amnesty International. Similarly, Monroy served for sixteen years as the president of the Spanish Evangelical Defense Commission, an interdenominational organization devoted to the defense of religious freedom in the country. Because of his expertise, he was called upon to help draft the law that allowed non-Catholic religious groups to establish permanent places of worship.[13] He also found time to write scholarly works on a variety of literary and religious subjects, including *La Biblia in El Quijote* (*The Bible in Don Quixote*) and *Albert Camus y El Protestantismo* (*Albert Camus and Protestantism*).[14] Most importantly for our purposes, while reporting on the 1964 New York World's Fair, Monroy stopped by the Protestant pavilion and met Tom Isaac, a minister of the Churches of Christ. The men studied the Bible together for several days, and though Isaac soon had to return to his congregation in New Orleans, the meeting brought Monroy into the Churches of Christ, an affiliation which continues to this day.[15]

In 1975, Ernesto Estevez, who had remained in Cuba, began a correspondence with Monroy, who was by that time working for the Churches of Christ-affiliated evangelistic organization Herald of Truth and editing a Spanish-language religious periodical, *Restauracion*. Monroy had long harbored a desire to preach on the island, but his attempts to enter the country had always been rebuffed by the Cuban government; "As an ex-Communist turned

---

13. Monroy, *An Autobiography*, 97–100, 146.

14. "Bibliografia," https://juanantoniomonroy.eicpos.com/bibliografia-2/.

15. Monroy, *An Autobiography*, 121–124.

Christian journalist," his presence was not greatly desired.[16] But, in 1985, in his capacity as a journalist, Monroy was invited to the inauguration of the new Nicaraguan president, Daniel Ortega. This led to a fateful encounter with Fidel Castro, which Monroy recounted in his autobiography:

> The opportunity presented itself one afternoon when I saw Fidel talking with the Catholic bishop Antonio Vega, president of the Bishop Conference in Nicaragua. There were a few people around them. I approached Castro and, interrupting the conversation, I said, "Mr. President, may I ask you a question?"
>
> He looked at me intensively with a piercing look, and then asked without much interest: "Who are you, boy?"
>
> "I'm Juan Antonio Monroy, Spanish reporter."
>
> "And what do you want to ask?"
>
> "I want to know why there isn't religious freedom in Cuba."
>
> If a look could kill, I wouldn't be writing this right now. The sharpness in his eyes announced his anger. Three bodyguards were very close to him. Fidel's look was a look that could penetrate from afar, like the smell of freshly cut grass. He let the words out with a military accent:
>
> "If you think there isn't religious freedom in Cuba, come and see for yourself."
>
> The bodyguards were getting close to me. My heart was beating harder than normal. I said one last thing:
>
> "I want to do that, Mr. President. I want to go to Cuba, but your embassy in Madrid won't give me a visa."

---

16. Archer, "What Can't Be Embargoed."

This time, he answered a little more relaxed, without anger: "Try again."[17]

Fidel, perhaps not understanding the full scope of Monroy's plans for the island, kept his word, and Monroy made his first trip to Cuba in March 1987. Upon his arrival, he met first with the leaders of the Havana congregation and then with those of seven other churches that had held on through the Castro era.[18] In the following years, Monroy returned to the island over fifty times, and eventually, Christians from the United States followed suit. Youth, men's, and women's conferences were established in the late 1990s, as well as a Herald of Truth-sponsored radio program. And perhaps most dramatically representative of the changing fortunes of the Churches of Christ in Cuba, the fellowship was allowed to use the National Capitol Building in Havana for a regional preachers' meeting, which brought together over five hundred ministers.

The other Stone-Campbell Movement fellowships are also once again represented among the island's churches. The Disciples of Christ have established a working relationship with Cuban Pentecostals. The independent Christian Churches have built up their own network of *casas cultos*, or house churches, as well as the Be Ye Reconciled to God Bible Institute.[19] The International Churches of Christ

---

17. Monroy, *An Autobiography*, 166–167.
18. The stories of many of these Cuban Christians have yet to be preserved, but an important step has been taken with Bobby Ross Jr., "For Cuba, a time of stress—and salvation," *Christian Chronicle*, November 14, 2023, https://christianchronicle.org/for-cuba-a-time-of-stress-and-salvation/, as well as the accompanying episode (51) of the *Christian Chronicle Podcast*, which includes a conversation between Ross Jr., Fernandez, and Archer.
19. Fernandez and Archer, *A History of Churches of Christ in Cuba*, 15.

have maintained a clandestine presence, too, with an underground gathering (likely based in Havana) numbering in the fifties by the early 2000s.[20]

A small but meaningful measure of political influence, a widely-heard radio program, a membership numbering roughly five thousand people worshipping across more than one hundred congregations: while one might be tempted to ask, along with Derek Cooper, "How would Christianity look differently had Cuba never encountered communism and the Protestants grew in popularity?"[21] the Churches of Christ have, at least, clawed their way back to their pre-Castro strength in the years following Juan Antonio Monroy's ambush of *El Comandante*.

---

20. C. Foster Stanback, *Into All Nations: A History of the International Churches of Christ* (Newton Upper Falls, MA: Illumination Publishers International, 2005), 167. The names of congregations in areas of ongoing state persecution, such as Cuba and the DPRK, are replaced by codenames in the charts Stanback provides. However, the ICOC approach to overseas evangelization was to target major and capital cities first, so it is probable that the sole Cuban congregation listed was in Havana.

21. Cooper, *Introduction to World Christian History*, 159.

Chapter 2

"A Model Military Document"

T.B. Larimore and the Battle of Shiloh

I'VE NEVER HAD the same fascination with the American Civil War that many historians, professional or otherwise, share, but I do have fond memories of visiting the Shiloh National Military Park several times over the course of my thirty-five (and counting) years. My dad took me to the site of the battle for the first time when I was three, or so I'm told, and we've been back a few times since then. I also went twice on high school field trips and have done my fair share of academic and popular reading on the battle. I'm not an expert, necessarily, but not a complete novice, either.

My primary area of research as a historian is the history and theology of the Stone-Campbell Movement, and my first major research undertaking was an article on T.B. Larimore, which was eventually published in *Restoration Quarterly* back in 2016.[1] My fascination with Larimore stems in part from my thirteen years at Mars Hill Bible School

---

1. John Young, "Dixieland's Demise: T.B. Larimore's Dixieland College and the Tenuous Position of Christian Colleges within the Churches of Christ," *Restoration Quarterly* 58. 3 (2016): 143–159.

(kindergarten through twelfth grade) but also from a copy of *Life, Letters, and Sermons of T.B. Larimore* that my better half gifted me back in 2013. At that point, I was just beginning my master's degree in history and wasn't sure what kind of research I wanted to pursue. The timely, perhaps even providential, gift steered me toward SCM history, and the rest, well, was history.

Life, Letters, and Sermons obviously proved to be a work of great importance for my career, but I was always a bit perplexed by an anecdote related early in the book by the author, Emma Page Larimore, T.B.'s second wife. T.B. served as a scout in the Confederate army, though he was eventually captured in 1863 and sent back home after taking the noncombatant oath. Prior to that time, however, Larimore saw action at the Battle of Shiloh, and on that topic, Emma Page writes:

> The memory of those war experiences was very vivid in his mind. He was with the army at the battle of Shiloh, the duty assigned to him being to watch the Tennessee River for the appearance of Federal gunboats; and he wrote the dispatch that informed General Albert Sydney Johnston of the presence on the river of two gunboats convoying a fleet of transports up the river—a dispatch that General Johnston pronounced "a model military document." When we visited Shiloh National Park a few years ago, Mr. Larimore searched for, and, with the help of a citizen of that community, found the spot on the river where he caught his first glimpse of the gunboats. He said there was a house just behind him on the high bluff on which he was lying as he watched the river, and in a thicket of berry vines we found the remains of the chim-

neys of the house that stood just where he remembered it to have been."[2]

EMMA PAGE

Emma Page

Several details of the above story can be easily confirmed. As noted already, Larimore was a Confederate scout, so this type of assignment would not have been unusual for him.[3] The gunboats mentioned in the quotation were an important feature of the Shiloh battle, providing covering fire that prevented the Federal position from being overrun at the end of a disastrous first day.[4] The broad

2. Mrs. T.B. (Emma Page) Larimore, *Life, Letters, and Sermons of T.B. Larimore* (Nashville, TN: Gospel Advocate Company, 1931), 12.

3. Douglas A. Foster, "Larimore, Theophilus Brown (1843–1929)," in *The Encyclopedia of the Stone-Campbell Movement*, eds. Douglas A. Foster et al (Grand Rapids, MI: Eerdmans, 2004), 452–453.

4. The presence of the gunboats is mentioned in numerous histories of the Shiloh battle, but they also made the cut for the relevant volume of the Oxford History of the United States. See James M. McPherson, *Battle Cry*

outlines of Larimore's Confederate service and his memories of it are simple enough to trace as well. According to historian Wes Crawford, Larimore spoke often of his Confederate service, which "helped perpetuate the memory of the Confederacy ... his speech reveals his great pride in being counted among the Confederate veterans."[5]

However, a feasible timeline for the story is harder to identify, as Johnston's death in the early afternoon of the first day of battle considerably shortens the window in which he could have read a message from Larimore. Johnston was shot in the leg around 2:10 pm, but he seemed generally unconcerned about the incident and did not seek treatment for what likely would have been a survivable wound—with a doctor's assistance. In the end, he was declared dead around 2:30 pm, leaving P.G.T. Beauregard as the ranking officer for the remainder of the battle.[6]

---

of Freedom: The Civil War Era (New York: Oxford University Press, 1988), 412.

5. Wes Crawford, "Churches of Christ and Lost Cause Religion: One Southern Denomination's Attempt to Find Identity in Post-Civil War America," *Restoration Quarterly* 64.1 (2022): 11.

6. O. Edward Cunningham, *Shiloh and the Western Campaign of 1862*, eds. Gary D. Joiner and Timothy B. Smith (New York: Savas Beatie LLC, 2007), 273–276. Also helpful in reconstructing the timeline of the Shiloh battle, including Johnston's death, is Smith's work *Rethinking Shiloh: Myth and Memory* (Knoxville, TN: University of Tennessee Press, 2013).

Albert Sydney Johnston

Further complicating the timeline is that the two gunboats–the *Lexington* and the *Tyler*—had been effectively out of the battle for most of the day because of a lack of clear orders from on high. "After listening to the sounds of battle for a good while," one historian notes, the commanding officer of the *Tyler* started to move into position to support a possible Federal retreat, while the *Lexington* moved back to the location where it had started the day. "Occasionally Confederate overshots splashed water around" the *Tyler*, but even with its closer position, it was simply sitting still on the water, and it was not clear that any Confederates were aware of its location at that time. Finally, around 1:25 pm, the commanding officer sent a subordinate ashore to find some updated orders for the ship, and after his return, the *Tyler* started shelling the Confederate army around 2:50 pm, almost half an hour after Johnston's death.[7] By the time the first of the gunboats entered the fray, then, Johnston was no longer around to read any dispatches.

This is far from a thorough debunking of the story, but it does raise some questions as to whether a message about the gunboats' entry into the battle could have been delivered on the day of battle in time for Johnston to compliment Larimore on his writing. To be sure, reconstructing timelines for battles is always a tricky business, and there is the possibility that Larimore's missive related to an earlier Confederate encounter with the *Lexington* and *Tyler* a few days before the start of the battle proper.[8] This interpretation is supported by a slightly different account of Larimore's involvement at Shiloh, also written by Emma Page Larimore but published roughly twenty years earlier:

> He was at the battle of Shiloh, but was in command of a special picket detachment detailed to watch the river above Pittsburg Landing and report all movements of the Federals that might be observed. He wrote the dispatch that informed Gen. Albert Sidney Johnston of the arrival and presence of the first Federal gunboats and transports above Pittsburg Landing, where the Federals who fought at Shiloh landed ....[9]

7. Cunningham, *Shiloh and the Western Campaign of 1862*, 312–313.

8. Cunningham, *Shiloh and the Western Campaign of 1862*, 116.

9. Emma Page (Larimore), *Letters and Sermons of T.B. Larimore*, vol. 3 (McQuiddy Printing Company, 1910), 286–287.

Sunken Road, Shiloh National Park

This version places T.B. on the scene prior to the battle, observing the Federal troops arriving at Pittsburg Landing in advance of the main conflict, which would have given plenty of time for him to write a noteworthy dispatch to his general. This, to me, seems to be the most likely version of events, but the other question remains: is there any evidence that Johnston spoke so highly of his scout's writing?

My initial guess had been that Larimore's memory had gotten a bit foggy with age and that the anecdote from *Life, Letters, and Sermons* might have been an embellishment of an actual, original event made grander by time. That volume, after all, was not published until 1931, nearly seventy years after the events of the battle. The other quotation cited above was published in 1910, closing the gap somewhat but still leaving nearly fifty years for the story to have developed or changed.

Another find moves the date for the anecdote much closer to the purported event, though there is still no evidence cited for the source. In his 1889 work *Smiles and Tears: Or, Larimore and His Boys*, F.D. Srygley offers the following version of events, much closer in substance to the earlier of the two Emma Page Larimore recountings:

He was at the battle of Shiloh, and was put in command of a special picket squad to guard the river above Pittsburg, to prevent a flank movement by Federals landing at a point higher up the river. He wrote the dispatch which gave Johnson [sic] notice of the passage of the first Federal gun-boat above Pittsburg. Johnson is said to have remarked that the dispatch was a model military document.[10]

Although Srygley's account doesn't establish a timeline, the substance of Larimore's orders seems to fit well with the version offered two decades later by Emma Page, and again seems to confirm that his message was related to events prior to, rather than from, the battle proper. Yet we have no source for the Johnston remark, and this is, as best as I can tell, the earliest version of the story in print—over two and a half decades after the fact. Srygley simply tells us that Johnston "is said to have remarked," but the vague, passive nature of the sentence does little to indicate how Larimore, or Srygley for that matter, might have heard the remark. Perhaps Larimore delivered the missive himself, or a courier brought word back to him later. We simply don't know.

In the end, then, we have a plausible set of circumstances for Larimore to have written a "model military document" a few days prior to the battle itself, but no clear way to establish how the purported compliment might have gotten back around to him. Sometimes, as historians, our sources don't provide us everything we might hope for, and that seems to be the case this time.

---

10. F.D. Srygley, *Smiles and Tears: Or, Larimore and His Boys* (F.D. Srygley, 1889), 72.

Chapter 3

"They better bring a wheelbarrow"
Austin McGary and the KKK

A SIMILAR DIFFICULTY arises in trying to verify an unusual story about Churches of Christ preacher, editor, sheriff, and both former member and noted opponent of the Ku Klux Klan, Austin McGary. Born on February 6, 1846, in Huntsville, Texas,[1] McGary (like Larimore) joined the Confederate military at a young age—so young, in fact, that he was still only nineteen at the war's end.[2] Four years after being paroled from the defeated army at Houston, McGary killed a man in Midway, though his legal defense of self-defense ultimately proved successful.[3] Around the age of

---

1. F.D. Srygley, *Biographies and Sermons: A Collection of Original Sermons by Different Men, with a Biographical Sketch of Each Man Accompanying His Sermon, Illustrated by Half-Tone Cuts*, (Nashville, TN: Gospel Advocate, 1961), 358.

2. Many of the dates in this section come from the timeline compiled by Terry Gardner at "Austin McGary," *The Restoration Movement*, https://www.therestorationmovement.com/_states/texas/mcgary,austin.htm, hereafter referred to as the "Gardner timeline."

3. Terry J. Gardner, "McGary, Austin (1846–1928)," in *The Encyclopedia of the Stone-Campbell Movement*, eds. Douglas A. Foster et. al (Grand Rapids, MI: Eerdmans, 2004), 507–508.

thirty, McGary became the sheriff of Madison County, Texas, a post which he held for about two years.[4] During his tenure, McGary killed a suspect who had tried to outdraw him. Perhaps because of dangers like these, McGary later moved into a similar role as a prisoner transport for the state of Texas, a job which he likewise held for about two years. Still a religious skeptic at this point, McGary returned to Madison County to reconsider his future.[5]

Austin McGary

On December 24, 1881, McGary was baptized just before the year's end; he soon pursued his newfound religious calling with the same dedication (and wanderlust) that he had shown during his time in law enforcement. In 1883,

---

4. Srygley, *Biographies and Sermons*, 360.
5. Srygley, *Biographies and Sermons*, 360–361; Earl Irvin West, *The Search for the Ancient Order: A History of the Restoration Movement*, vol. 2, *1866–1906* (Indianapolis: Religious Book Service, 1950), 403.

McGary relocated to Austin, from which he began publishing the *Firm Foundation* during the following year.[6] Never content to stay put for long, though, McGary lived in at least six different Texas communities between 1891 and 1897, according to Lane Cubstead, and he even evinced interest in establishing a colony in Mexico around 1900.[7] Eventually losing control of the *Firm Foundation* in 1902, for reasons doctrinal and otherwise, McGary moved several more times in the following years, including stays in Los Angeles, California; Eugene, Oregon; and Springdale, Arkansas, where he purchased a farm. By the 1910s at the latest, McGary had landed back in Texas, from where he would edit several religious and prohibitionist papers in the next few years before passing away on June 15, 1928, in Houston.[8]

This summary has hardly done justice to the larger-than-life story of Austin McGary. Earl Irvin West observes in the second volume of *The Search for the Ancient Order* that McGary's stories helped inspire John W. Thomason Jr.'s novel *The Lone Star Preacher*, and even the usually restrained West devotes an entire chapter to McGary and the exciting, though often uncited, stories of his adventures.[9] In fact, it is one of those stories that I wanted to investigate since it has, like the above tale about Larimore,

6. West, *Search for the Ancient Order* vol. 2, 403; Srygley, *Biographies and Sermons*, 361; Gardner timeline.

7. Lane Cubstead, "History as the Firm Foundation Made It," *Firm Foundation*, April 28, 1959, 259; Earl Irvin West, *The Search for the Ancient Order: A History of the Restoration Movement*, vol. 3, *1900–1918* (Indianapolis: Religious Book Service, 1979), 362.

8. Gardner timeline.

9. West, *Search for the Ancient Order* vol. 2, 397. The chapter continues through p. 408.

shown up in numerous works on McGary in the years since his death. West's account of the incident is as follows:

> The most prominent characteristic of McGary was his courage. Fear had absolutely no part in his make-up. At Willis, Texas, near Houston, the Ku-Klux Klan became active after the Civil War, and McGary was widely recognized as a bitter enemy. He was warned to get out of Willis, but he ignored the warning, until a stranger from another town informed him that he would be killed, and that people from another community would do it if he did not move. McGary was puzzled for a moment what to do. He conceived a plan, and sent an old Negro to every street corner in the town to shout at the top of his voice that McGary would speak on a certain Sunday afternoon at a specified locality on the subject of "Ku-Klux Klan."
>
> The time arrived and the town was full of people. McGary laid serious charges before the Klan. The Klan was unconstitutional. He related how they had taken an old preacher out of his house at night and beaten him unmercifully. McGary's language was bitter in the extreme. He told them his door was unlocked at all times; that they could come any time they choose, but they better bring a wheelbarrow in which to haul their boys off. "I have a gun and some of you know that I am handy with it," McGary cried. The Ku-Klux Klan never bothered A. McGary.[10]

Although I must have initially encountered this story many years ago when reading West for the first time, it was only with the much more recent publication of Jason Fikes's

---

10. West, *Search for the Ancient Order* vol. 2, 404–405.

2022 article "Jesse P. Sewell, White Supremacy, and the Formative Years of Abilene Christian College" that it jumped out to me. In that article, Fikes summarizes the above anecdote, citing West, and adds that "Later in 1923, McGary wrote an extended editorial to the *Houston Chronicle* denouncing the Klan's unlawful and cowardly activities."[11] This editorial has, thanks to the work of Terry Gardner and John Mark Hicks, been reproduced on Hicks's website; in it, McGary forthrightly discusses both his previous involvement with the Klan during the Reconstruction era as well as the reasons for his later opposition to it.[12]

As you may have guessed already, however, I am more interested in the bit about the wheelbarrow. This aspect of McGary's anti-Klan activity is much harder to verify: Fikes cites West, but West cites no one! The dearth of citations in West's McGary chapter has already been identified and explored at length in a helpful post by Terry Gardner in the "Friends of the Restoration" Facebook group, which fact-checks the widely repeated but erroneous claims that McGary never carried a gun, or killed anyone, or both.[13]

Since West also does not give a date for the story in question, we must first try to figure out when it could have taken place, if indeed it did. Two options jump to the top of the list. The first extrapolates from the dates given by West for other milestones in McGary's life and assumes that the

---

11. Jason Fikes, "Jesse P. Sewell, White Supremacy, and the Formative Years of Abilene Christian College," *Restoration Quarterly* 64.3 (2022): 176.

12. Republished as "A Stone-Campbell 'Father' on the Ku Klux Klan," https://johnmarkhicks.com/2011/12/31/a-stone-campbell-father-on-the-ku-klux-klan/.

13. Terry Gardner, "Austin McGary and Internet Quotations," in "Friends of the Restoration" Facebook group, November 3, 2021.

historian slotted the story into the appropriate place in the narrative, even though he did not call attention to it. This would place the story somewhere in the vicinity of 1883–1884, between McGary's move to Austin and his founding of the *Firm Foundation*.

This hypothesis has several definite drawbacks, however. While nothing in West's version of events necessarily requires McGary to have been living in Willis at the time of the confrontation, it seems less than likely that he would have moved to Austin in 1883, started his paper in the same town in 1884, but have also spent enough time in Willis in the meantime to provoke such hostility from the Klan—especially since Willis is much closer to Houston, where McGary also lived for several years, than to Austin.

A stronger option places the potential Willis incident at some point in the very early 1920s, just prior to the aforementioned *Houston Chronicle* editorial. In that piece, McGary states that he had decided previously not to speak publicly about the Klan "again," although circumstances had forced a change of plans. A.R. Holton places McGary in Willis during the 1920s,[14] and the McGary-Douglas debate locates in Willis at the time of the discussion in 1921.[15] Though this timeline doesn't square with West's implied chronology, it is a much more feasible window for the incident to have occurred, and it would also explain the

14. A.R. Holton, "75 Years Advancing With Texas," *Firm Foundation*, January 20, 1959, 38.

15. The debate was published in serial form in *The Apostolic Way* beginning with the January 15, 1921 issue, and all three pieces (April 1, 1921, and October 1, 1921, are the other two) have McGary posting his correspondence from Willis. Eventually, the work was compiled into a book, the full citation for which is given in Michael W. Casey, "From Religious Outsiders to Insiders: The Rise and Fall of Pacifism in the Churches of Christ," *Journal of Church and State* 44.3 (Summer 2002): 464 n47.

strong (even by McGary's standards) rhetoric in the *Houston Chronicle* editorial.

Even with this more plausible timeline for the Willis confrontation, however, we still need to evaluate (in the absence of any primary source evidence prior to West's chapter) how believable the story is. To be sure, the ideas that McGary would stage a public scene of this nature, that he would threaten violence if someone challenged him, and that he would be strongly opposed to the Klan in these later years of his life are all reasonable; there is nothing in the story that immediately jumps out as being out of character for McGary. However, West's version is very light on details; in addition to the missing time frame, none of the other participants in the story besides McGary is identified, and neither is the "other town" from which the specter of violence was emanating. It sounds like a preacher story—it's interesting, it gives us a feel for McGary as an individual, but even though it tells us truth in the abstract sense, it may or may not do so in a more literal way.

Chapter 4

Unity in Church and Country

Exploring the Lincoln-Larimore Rumor

GROWING UP IN FLORENCE, Alabama, and attending Mars Hill Bible School from kindergarten through twelfth grade, I occasionally heard a rumor floated that Abraham Lincoln—yes, that one—was the father of preacher, teacher, and Mars Hill founder T.B. Larimore. This lineage was always proposed as a "Wouldn't it be interesting if this were true?" hypothesis rather than propounded as a "This is true" statement, but the idea seemed so bizarre to me even at the time that I just filed it away as a curiosity and moved on with life. However, as you can tell from the assortment of chapters included in this book, I've spent a fair bit of time recently thinking about the connections, such as they are, between the Stone-Campbell Movement and the American presidency. I've also been deep in Larimore-related research for another ongoing book project. As such, I decided to see if I could figure out the source of the rumor and what truth, if any, may rest underneath it all.

Presidential Candidate Abraham Lincoln, 1860
(Thomas Hicks - Leopold Grozelier)

As it turns out, the Lincoln-as-Larimore's-father hypothesis can be easily dismissed simply by doing some birthday math. At first glance, admittedly, the math does not seem quite so conclusive. T.B. Larimore was born on July 10, 1843; his mother, Nancy, was 30 at the time. Too, Abraham Lincoln was a contemporary of Nancy's, having been born in early 1809, just under four years earlier. Could the future president, a native of neighboring Kentucky, have secretly fathered one of the most important figures in Stone-Campbell Movement history?

No. According to the Lehrman Institute's "Abraham Lincoln's Classroom" project, "Abraham Lincoln never visited Tennessee—except perhaps as a young man while rafting down the Mississippi River to New Orleans."[1]

---

1. "Abraham Lincoln and Tennessee," *The Lehrman Institute Presents: Abraham Lincoln's Classroom,* https://www.abrahamlincolnsclassroom. org/abraham-lincoln-state-by-state/abraham-lincoln-and-tennessee.

Glenn W. LaFantasie, writing for the *Friends of the Lincoln Collection*, adds that

> In his youth, Abraham Lincoln took two trips down the Mississippi River on flatboats laden with goods to be sold in New Orleans. The first trip occurred in the spring of 1828, when Lincoln lived in Indiana and agreed to accompany Allen Gentry, a merchant's son, down the Ohio River and the Mississippi to the Crescent City, the fat southern market city where westerners knew they could get top dollar for anything from pork to corn whiskey, tobacco to sorghum.
>
> The second flatboat journey happened a few years later, in April 1831, when Lincoln, who had recently arrived in Illinois and gone off on his own, compared himself to "a sort of floting Drift wood."[2]

In short, the only two times Lincoln was ever in Tennessee, if indeed he happened to get off the boat there on either occasion, were well over a decade before T.B. Larimore was born. This is to say nothing of the vast geographic distance between the Mississippi River and the eastern Tennessee area where T.B. was born and raised.

The Lincoln-Larimore connection is nothing more than rumor-mongering, then, but where did the rumor start, and why? In the process of reconstructing the above timeline, I came across a quotation in the work of another historian that answers those questions, yet in the process offers

---

2. Glenn W. LaFantasie, "The Mystery of Lincoln's Second Flatboat Trip to New Orleans," *Friends of the Lincoln Collection*, https://www. friendsofthelincolncollection.org/lincoln-lore/the-mystery-of-lincolns-second-flatboat-trip-to-new-orleans/.

another president as a potential candidate to investigate. Observing T.B.'s warmth towards his mother and silence regarding his father, Earl Kimbrough writes that

> James R. Cope, Jr., then president of Florida College and a native of White County Tennessee, told the writer in 1976 that older preachers in Tennessee, contemporary with Larimore, believed the story that circulated about him to the effect that Larimore's father was Andrew Johnson, a tailor of Greenville, Tennessee, for whom Larimore's mother worked as a young girl. Johnson later became famous as the U.S. senator from Tennessee who sided with the federal government when his state seceded from the Union at the outbreak of the Civil War. Johnson served as Military Governor of Tennessee during the war, vice president in Abraham Lincoln's brief second administration, and the sixteenth president upon Lincoln's assassination. This is inserted here because it is omitted from the extant works on Larimore written by his friends. If true, and it may not be, it would only add to the stature of the man who rose from such ignoble beginnings to become one of the greatest gospel evangelists of the nineteenth and twentieth centuries.[3]

Kimbrough's final sentence in this section seems to indicate a level of skepticism ("If true, and it may not be"), but the paragraph does give us some crucial information about how rumors of T.B.'s presidential parentage originated and survived down to the present day (preacher gossip) and puts

---

3. Earl Kimbrough, *The Warrior from Rock Creek: Life, Times, and Thoughts of F.B. Srygley, 1859–1940* (Louisville, KY: Religious Supply Center, 2008), 42–43.

forth a father figure who initially seems much more plausible than Lincoln.

Andrew Johnson

The North Carolina-born tailor and politician Andrew Johnson was only a few years older than Nancy Lincoln. Born in late 1808, Johnson moved with his family to Greeneville, Tennessee, in 1826, becoming a tailor upon arrival in his new city.[4] The following year, he married Eliza McCardle, and while the couple remained married until Andrew's death in 1875, the marriage was not always a close one. The two were routinely separated by Andrew's political travels, which Eliza's inconsistent health frequently prevented her from joining. Additionally, while running for a seat in the U.S. House of Representatives,

4. Elizabeth R. Varon, "Andrew Johnson: Life Before the Presidency," *UVA Miller Center*, https://millercenter.org/president/johnson/life-before-the-presidency.

Johnson was accused in 1872 of having an affair with the wife of a neighbor and fellow tailor. Knoxville newspapers that year reported that James W. Harold had received an anonymous letter claiming that Johnson and his wife, Emily Wright Harold, had been carrying on an affair. Whether anything took place or not has been the subject of considerable debate, both then and now, but regardless, the story had a tragic ending, with Emily dying of gunshot wounds, likely self-inflicted, on May 8, 1872.[5]

Johnson's longtime residence in Tennessee, his profession as a tailor, and the scandal of possible infidelity all make him a slightly more believable candidate than Lincoln, but once again, under closer scrutiny, the timeline falls apart. According to Cope via Kimbrough's recollection, Nancy worked for Andrew Johnson as a "young girl." This is at least plausible, though I have found no evidence that Nancy ever worked in Greeneville, which is several hundred miles from the Sequatchie Valley where she lived while T.B. was growing up. But as we noted above, Nancy was thirty years old when T.B. was born—not old by any stretch, but hardly a "young girl." Additionally, Andrew Johnson was elected to the Tennessee Senate in 1841 and then to the U.S. House of Representatives in 1843. Although his political career did take him away from Greeneville for extended periods of time, it did so in the

---

5. Delonda Anderson, "Hidden Scandal: a Woman, a Gun, and a President," *Appalachia Bare*, August 17, 2021, https://www.appalachiabare. com/hidden-scandal-a-woman-a-gun-and-a-president/. Anderson makes the case that Emily was murdered, perhaps to put a lid on the brewing scandal. Whether one agrees with this interpretation of the evidence, Anderson does an excellent job of unpacking the context of the election and the relationship between the Johnsons and the Harolds.

directions of Nashville and Washington, not of rural east Tennessee.

As interesting as it would be for one of the most notable Restoration Movement leaders of the late nineteenth and early twentieth centuries to be the son of a United States president, all available evidence indicates otherwise. Research regarding the identity of Larimore's actual father is still ongoing, but based on the above timelines, at least two possibilities can be removed from the list.

Chapter 5

A Bible in One Hand, The Constitution in the Other

The Stone-Campbell Movement and the American Presidency

AT THE VERY end of the book which emerged from my dissertation research, I briefly mentioned the presence of restorationist themes in American political rhetoric[1] and noted that this might be a fruitful avenue for future research. Although my research agenda has, for the most part, gone in a different direction since then, I have had a couple of opportunities to write and present smaller pieces on the intersection of politics and the Stone-Campbell Movement. This chapter is an attempt to pull those threads together by considering, first, which American presidents had meaningful historical ties to the movement, and second, looking for evidence of restorationist rhetoric in the speeches and writings of some of those figures.

Of the three bona fide Stone-Campbell Movement-affiliated presidents, James Garfield, who is undergoing some-

---

1. This is not unique to the U.S., to be sure, as evidenced by the research presented in Jason H. Dormady, *Primitive Revolution: Restorationist Religion and the Idea of the Mexican Revolution, 1940–1968* (Albuquerque, NM: University of New Mexico Press, 2011).

thing of a renaissance at the moment with a splashy new biography[2] and forthcoming Netflix series,[3]

James Garfield

is the most heavily indebted to the movement's theology.[4] His faith and its impact on the course of his career has already been thoroughly addressed in former Pepperdine historian Jerry Rushford's doctoral dissertation, tellingly named "The Political Disciple: The Relationship Between

---

2. C.W. Goodyear, *President Garfield: From Radical to Unifier* (New York: Simon & Schuster, 2023).

3. Tara Bitran and Phillipe Thao, "Everything to Know About Benioff and Weiss' *Death by Lightning*," https://www.netflix.com/tudum/articles/death-by-lightning-tv-series-adaptation.

4. For more on the three movement-affiliated presidents and the ways in which their beliefs impacted their politics, see the chapters in section three, "The Influence of a Tradition on the Presidency," in Michael W. Casey and Douglas A. Foster, eds., *The Stone-Campbell Movement: An International Religious Tradition* (Knoxville, TN: University of Tennessee Press, 2002), 217–268.

James A. Garfield and the Disciples of Christ," so I won't belabor the point here.[5] Despite his rather uncouth manner of speaking, Lyndon Johnson was a longtime member of the Disciples of Christ as well, a regular worshiper at the National City Christian Church, and part of a multi-generational movement family that even included a member of the Christadelphians.[6] And although he had already left the movement by the time he reached the White House, Ronald Reagan was raised in a home that included a devout Disciple mother, attended the Disciples-affiliated Eureka College, and maintained a friendship with Pat Boone, the famous singer and entertainer (and fellow political conservative) from Churches of Christ.[7]

---

5. Jerry Bryant Rushford, "Political Disciple: The Relationship Between James A. Garfield and the Disciples of Christ" (PhD diss., University of California Santa Barbara, 1977), https://digitalcommons.pepperdine.edu/heritage_center/7/.

6. Gregg Cantrell, "Lyndon's Granddaddy: Samuel Ealy Johnson Sr., Texas Populism, and the Improbable Roots of American Liberalism," *Southwestern Historical Quarterly* 118.2 (October 2014): 132–156; Philip A. Walker Jr., "Lyndon B. Johnson's Senate Foreign Policy Activism: The Suez Canal Crisis, a Reappraisal," *Presidential Studies Quarterly* 26.4 (Fall 1996): 996–1008.

7. See John M. Jones and Michael W. Casey, "Ronald Reagan, the Disciples of Christ, and Restoring America," in *And the WORD Became Flesh: Studies in History, Communication, and Scripture in Memory of Michael W. Casey*, eds. Thomas H. Olbricht and David Fleer (Eugene, OR: Pickwick Publications, 2009), 196–212, an essay to which we will return later.

Pat Boone

The three men each took different influences from their Stone-Campbell Movement heritage into the Oval Office and reached varying conclusions about how best to integrate their faith and their politics, but the effect of the movement's teachings is apparent in the lives and legacies of each.

Three other presidents also bear mentioning here, albeit for somewhat different reasons. Though the controversial statements of its pastor, the Reverend Jeremiah Wright Jr., led Barack Obama to break away from the Trinity United Church of Christ during the 2008 election season, the president had long had close ties to the congregation and to the broader tradition of which it is part.[8]

---

8. Carl A. Grant and Shelby J. Grant, *The Moment: Barack Obama, Jeremiah Wright, and the Firestorm at Trinity United Church of Christ* (Lanham, MD: Rowman & Littlefield Publishers, 2013).

Barack Obama (2005)

The Churches of Christ and the United Church of Christ are not as close in faith or practice as the similar names might suggest, but there is a meaningful historical link between the two groups if one goes far enough back. The "United" part of the UCC's name is a reference to the numerous mergers of various streams and traditions that have led to the present-day denomination. In 1957, three groups, including the General Council of the Congregational Christian Churches, consolidated into the current UCC. That General Council was itself the result of a merger of three smaller groups, which included the Christian Connection, or Connexion. Those with some familiarity with early Restoration Movement history will recognize the name of that group, which, of course, was connected with notable figures like Abner Jones, Elias Smith, James O'Kelly, and—most important for our purposes here—the followers of Barton W. Stone who did *not* find common ground with Alexander Campbell and who did *not* participate in the 1832 merger with those in his orbit.[9]

Barton W. Stone

In total, then, we have three Stone-Campbell Movement presidents and if you want to stretch the boundaries, a fourth Stone Movement commander-in-chief.

The other two presidents that bear mentioning here are included solely for the purposes of myth-busting. Rumors have long swirled about the supposed "secret baptisms" of George Washington and Abraham Lincoln. That the two would be the subjects of such speculation is understandable; Washington and Lincoln consistently score near or at the top of the all-time presidential rankings, and the religious views of both are shrouded in some degree of mystery. Presidential historian Gary Scott Smith writes in *Faith and*

9. "History," United Church of Christ, https://www.ucc.org/who-we-are/about/history/.

the Presidency: From George Washington to George W. Bush that

> Like George Washington's, Lincoln's faith has been closely scrutinized, hotly debated, and often misunderstood. Both men attributed their success in war to divine providence, proclaimed days of public thanksgiving and prayer as president, rarely mentioned Jesus, and were intensely private about their personal beliefs.[10]

Another way in which the two are connected is in the popular perception that they underwent some sort of "secret baptism" which might tie them, directly or indirectly, to the Stone-Campbell Movement. For Washington, the story is that the Baptist chaplain John Gano baptized the future president during the famously trying winter at Valley Forge. John Gano was, of course, the great-grandfather of Richard M. Gano, the famous Stone-Campbell Movement preacher and Confederate general.[11] According to the story, which got its start in sworn affidavits given by descendants of John Gano, the chaplain baptized Washington in front of over forty witnesses because the general had concerns about the method, though not the purpose, of Episcopalian baptism.[12]

The question is not whether Washington was a member

---

10. Gary Scott Smith, *Faith and the Presidency; From George Washington to George W. Bush* (New York: Oxford University Press, 2006), 91.

11. Jerry Bryant Rushford, "'The Apollos of the West': The Life of John Allen Gano" (MA thesis, Abilene Christian College, 1972), gives more on the history of the Gano family and its deep connections to the movement.

12. Frank Richey, *Vignettes of Virtue: Short Stories of the American Restoration Movement* (Florence, AL: Cypress Creek Book Company, 2010), 108–109.

of the Restoration Movement, which he clearly wasn't, but whether the baptism took place. To that end, while one would not want to call into question Gano's descendants, who put their credibility on the line in testifying to the event, historians have long pointed out that there are several major problems with the story. For one, Gano was not a chaplain under Washington but under George Clinton, and he was not present at Valley Forge. Additionally, no first-hand witnesses ever came forward to verify the tale, and Gano makes no mention of the supposed baptism in his own writings. And though the story is commemorated in a famous painting now held at William Jewell College in Liberty, Missouri, the college itself does not even take a stance on the legend's veracity.[13]

The "secret baptism" of Washington, in fact, fits into a larger genre of dubious stories in which founding and other important figures of American history demonstrate a measure of piety that would, if true, bring them more fully into the nation's religious mainstream. This body of litera-ture includes a similarly apocryphal story (or rather, stories; each Christian group seems to have its own) about the supposed baptism of Abraham Lincoln. "Abraham Lincoln never claimed to be a member of any church," Jim Martin begins his 1996 exploration of the subject, "but almost every denomination makes some kind of claim" to him.[14] For the Disciples of Christ and the broader Stone-Campbell

---

13. Jacob Hicks, "The Legend of George Washington's Baptism," *Digital Encyclopedia of George Washington*, https://www.mountvernon.org/library/digitalhistory/digital-encyclopedia/article/the-legend-of-george-washington-s-baptism.

14. Jim Martin, "The Secret Baptism of Abraham Lincoln," *Restoration Quarterly* 38.2 (1996): 65–76. The quoted material comes specifically from page 65.

Movement, the story of Lincoln's baptism comes originally from a single source, G.M. Weimer. Piecing together several of his writings from 1942, when he was eighty-five and nearing the end of his life, Weimer, in totality, claimed that the former Illinois state evangelist, John O'Kane, had secretly immersed Lincoln in a creek to avoid upsetting Lincoln's wife. Weimer was living in Eureka, Illinois, at the time of this conversation with O'Kane while Weimer's sons were in college, and the fateful talk took place at a Disciples' state convention held there in the same town.

Unfortunately, as Martin points out, the more specific of these details complicate considerably the possible time-line of events. Given that O'Kane died in 1881 when Weimer was only twenty-four, it seems unlikely that Weimer would have been old enough to have two sons in college at that age. Too, the last time the Illinois state convention was held before O'Kane's death was in 1878, shifting the timeline three more years and making Weimer no older than twenty-one at the time of the ostensible meeting. Again, without wanting to portray ministers from past generations in an overly negative light, the story simply doesn't stand up to inquiry. (Lincoln's father and step-mother, Thomas and Sarah, did become members of the Disciples, but this was after the future president had moved out of the house, and Abraham was not at all close to his father and would not have seen him as a religious influence to be emulated.)

But it is one thing for a president to have a direct, personal connection to the Restoration Movement, and quite another for a president to rely on a political variant of restorationism to appeal to voters. The latter is far more common in practice, though discussion is not as prevalent in the scholarly literature as one might expect. A handful of exceptions argue that an appeal to the examples of the past could, paradoxically, be attached to a somewhat forward-looking political ideology. Nathan O. Hatch's seminal *The Democratization of American Christianity* argues that "Both [Joseph] Smith and [Alexander] Campbell were explicitly Jeffersonian in their hostility to the heavy hand of the past and perfectly in accord with Jeffersonian assumptions,"[15]

Alexander Campbell

while William Mervin Moorhouse's dissertation observes how Andrew Jackson and his followers "appealed to the 'restoration of ancestral order of things,' or a return to a 'wise and frugal government,' where the constitution is 'fundamental and sacred'" at the same time that they sought to protect the natural rights of the "common people" over against the government.[16] Less enthusiastically, John Fea

---

15. Nathan O. Hatch, *The Democratization of American Christianity* (New Haven, CT: Yale University Press, 1989), 169.

16. William Mervin Moorhouse, "The Restoration Movement: The

argues that Donald Trump's "Make America Great Again" slogan was and is part of "a playbook characterized by attempts to 'win back' or 'restore the culture.' It is a playbook grounded in a highly problematic interpretation of the relationship between Christianity and the American founding."[17]

And how could a concern for the past not constantly be in the mind of the American president? Forrest McDonald reflected three decades ago in *The American Presidency: An Intellectual History* that

> The president lives in a museum of the history of the presidency. When walking along the halls of the White House, the president is constantly reminded that Jefferson walked the same halls as he waited for news of negotiations with Napoleon, that Lincoln walked them when waiting for news from Antietam. When dining, the president never entirely escapes the realization that he is using the same silver that Madison and both Roosevelts used. The president understands that he is a member of a mystical fraternity, representing an unbroken chain of history and mythology, and knows that far into the future presidents will be aware that he was a link in that chain, and cannot avoid wondering what his place will be in their memory and in the nation's memory.[18]

One of the most important ways in which presidents

Rhetoric of Jacksonian Restorationism in a Frontier Religion" (PhD diss., Indiana University, 1967), 22–23, 29.

17. John Fea, *Believe Me: The Evangelical Road to Donald Trump* (Grand Rapids, MI: Eerdmans, 2018), 6–7.

18. Forrest McDonald, *The American Presidency: An Intellectual History* (Lawrence, KS: University Press of Kansas, 1994), 466–467.

have tried to shape that memory, of course, is through the written word. Theirs is not the only say in the matter, and books written by others about the presidency or individual presidents are not going away any time soon. Still, as Carlos Lozada, long of the *Washington Post*, contends, "if journalism is still history's first draft, then books remain the first draft of how we think about that history, how we seek our place in it."[19] This is no less true for the presidents themselves than for the rest of us.

The reigning expert on the authorial talents of the presidents is likely Craig Fehrman, who in 2020 completed a lengthy survey[20] and an equally hefty primary source collection of presidential writings.[21] The scope of Fehrman's work goes far beyond ours here, but the source collection does provide an opportunity to consider how the Stone-Campbell Movement (or simply Stone Movement, in the case of Obama) presidents might have employed the restoration motif in their own writings. A couple of caveats: first, James Garfield was obviously unable to write a post-presidency memoir, leaving Fehrman to excerpt only a brief childhood story from Garfield's "Notes for the Benefit of Biographers" in the source collection.[22] Second, Ronald Reagan's widespread use of restorationist imagery in his speeches (though not his memoirs) has already been analyzed at length in an excellent essay by John M. Jones

---

19. Carlos Lozada, *What Were We Thinking: A Brief Intellectual History of the Trump Era* (New York: Simon & Schuster, 2020), 6.

20. Craig Fehrman, *Author in Chief: The Untold Story of Our Presidents and the Books They Wrote* (New York: Avid Reader Press, 2020).

21. Craig Fehrman, ed., *The Best Presidential Writing from 1789 to the Present* (New York: Avid Reader Press, 2020).

22. Excerpt from James Garfield, "Notes for the Benefits of Biographers," in Fehrman, ed., *The Best Presidential Writing*, 158–160.

and Michael W. Casey. Those two scholars argue persuasively "that a sacred doctrine of restoration, advanced by the Disciples of Christ, served as a mythic template for a political doctrine of restoration for America, which saturates Reagan's political discourse over the many decades of his political career."[23]

What of LBJ and Obama, though? Fehrman criticizes Johnson for overly sanitizing what should have been a very colorful memoir[24] and spends little time exploring its content, but he does include several other examples of LBJ's writings in the primary source collection and is more charitably disposed toward them. The most historically minded of the selections is Johnson's 1965 Address on Voting Rights, in which the president directly frames the pursuit of civil rights in the light of the nation's founding documents and ideals.

> This was the first nation in the history of the world to be founded with a purpose. The great phrases of that purpose still sound in every American heart, north and south: "All men are created equal"— "government by the consent of the governed"— "give me liberty or give me death." Well, those are not just clever words, or those are not just empty theories. In their name Americans have fought and died for two centuries, and tonight around the

---

23. Jones and Casey, "Ronald Reagan," 196.
24. He remarks on p. 325 of *Author in Chief* that "At the start of his deadening and defensive memoir, Lyndon Johnson wrote, 'This is a book that only a president could have written.' The author was admitting more than he knew."

world they stand there as guardians of our liberty, risking their lives.[25]

Fehrman is also substantially more charitable to Obama's writings, describing the president himself as "literary" and pointing out that his first two books "nabbed endorsements from highbrow authors like Philip Roth and Toni Morrison."[26] The excerpts included in the source collection include, though, selections from four speeches: the famous 2004 DNC address, his statement on the Sandy Hook school shooting, a speech given in 2015 on the Selma to Montgomery marches, and most important for our purposes here, an address given during the controversy over the Reverend Jeremiah Wright. In that speech, Obama acknowledges the historical limitations of the Constitution —chiefly, the way it was tarnished by the "original sin" of slavery—but also points out that the Constitution itself is the solution to its own problems. "Of course, the answer to the slavery question was already embedded within our Constitution," he remarks, "a Constitution that had at its very core the ideal of equal citizenship under the law; a Constitution that promised its people liberty, and justice, and a union that could be and should be perfected over time."[27] Though not exactly a proof-texting use of the Constitution, Obama's rhetoric nevertheless finds guidance for the present day in the ideals espoused by the founding generation.

The first volume of Obama's presidential memoir, *A*

---

25. Lyndon Johnson, Address on Voting Rights (1965), in Fehrman, ed., *The Best Presidential Writing*, 346.
26. Fehrman, *Author in Chief*, 300.
27. Barack Obama, Address on the Reverend Wright Controversy (2008), in Fehrman, ed., *The Best Presidential Writing*, 435.

Promised Land, was also released in 2020, but not soon enough to be included in Fehrman's books. Obama's use of history in the memoir, especially in the early pages, strongly resembles the excerpts chosen by Fehrman. Noting that in practice the United States has not always lived up to its ideals, he nevertheless refuses to repudiate those values or the past historical figures who espoused them: America, along with its failings, "was [also] the Constitution and the Bill of Rights, crafted by flawed but brilliant thinkers who reasoned their way to a system at once sturdy and capable of change."[28]

Regardless of whether another person with ties to the Stone-Campbell Movement or one of its constituent streams makes it to the White House, it is almost certain that presidents and other politicians will continue to rely on the rhetoric of restoration to shape their visions, guide their policies, and appeal to voters. And whether they seek to "Make America Great Again" or point to the socially leveling founding values of "liberty and justice for all," those appeals to the pattern of the past will undoubtedly find a receptive audience among voters.

---

28. Barack Obama, *A Promised Land* (New York: Crown, 2020), 14.

Chapter 6

1915

The Year the Disciples Ruled the Court

FOR A GROUP that has at times been home to a strong, theologically rooted tradition of political nonparticipation,[1] the Stone-Campbell Movement has also had its fair share of representation in the highest echelons of the United States federal government. This includes the presidency, as we have already seen, as well as the legislature.[2] One aspect of the movement's political engagement that has not yet come under scrutiny, however, is its impact on the judiciary. Of the 112 men and women who have served on the United States Supreme Court, two Justices who happened to overlap on the Court in 1915 were members of the Disci-

---

1. For a brief introduction to this theological strand within Churches of Christ, see Richard T. Hughes and James L. Gorman, *Reviving the Ancient Faith: The Story of Churches of Christ in America*, 3rd ed. (Grand Rapids, MI: Eerdmans, 2024), 324–326.

2. Neal Coates and Sean Evans, "The Political Awakening: Members of the Church of Christ in Congress" (paper presented at Christian Scholars' Conference, Lubbock, TX, June 2019); Cheryl Mann Bacon, "Members of House, Senate have ties to Churches of Christ," *Christian Chronicle*, January 18, 2021, https://christianchronicle.org/members-of-house-senate-have-ties-to-churches-of-christ/.

ples of Christ. Though very different in temperament and time spent on the Court, Joseph Rucker Lamar and James Clark McReynolds both reflected in their lives and legal careers the geographical, cultural, and intellectual influences of the movement.

The slightly younger of the two Justices, the Georgian Joseph Rucker Lamar, was born on October 14, 1857, into a family that was politically and religiously distinguished. Joseph's father was the well-known Disciples minister and theologian J.S. Lamar (1829–1908), who served for many years in congregations in Georgia[3]

Justice Joseph R. Lamar

---

3.   According to his daughter-in-law (Clarinda Pendleton Lamar, *The Life of Joseph Rucker Lamar, 1857–1916* (New York: G.P. Putnam's Sons, 1926), 11–12), he was most closely associated with the congregation at Augusta; however, in a strange historical coincidence, he was followed at the Valdosta congregation by a minister named J.C. McReynolds. J. Edward Mosley, *Disciples of Christ in Georgia* (St. Louis, MO: The Bethany Press, 1954), 268–269.

and is best remembered for publishing an influential theological work, *The Organon of Scripture*, three years after Joseph was born.[4] Another Lamar family member, Mirabeau, served as president of the Republic of Texas from 1838–1841.[5] In fact, Joseph would not even be the first Supreme Court Justice from his own family, with his impressively named cousin Lucius Quintus Cincinnatus Lamar holding a spot on the bench from 1888–1893.[6]

Still, even in such an accomplished family, Joseph was recognized as a special talent, and his father pushed him hard. J.S. steered his son to Bethany College in 1875, and Joseph finished a course of study there two years later.[7] Along with knowledge, Joseph found romance during his undergraduate days. He fell in love with Clarinda Huntington Pendleton, daughter of Bethany president and noted Stone-Campbell Movement leader W.K. Pendleton. The couple married in early 1879, not long after Joseph had been admitted to the Georgia bar and begun his noteworthy legal and political career.[8]

4. Tim Sensing, "Lamar, James Sanford (1829–1908)," in Douglas A. Foster et al., eds., *The Encyclopedia of the Stone-Campbell Movement* (Grand Rapids, MI: Eerdmans, 2004), 449–450.

5. John W. Winkle III, "Lamar, Joseph Rucker," in James W. Ely and Joel B. Grossman, eds., *The Oxford Companion to the Supreme Court of the United States* (New York: Oxford University Press, 2005), 569.

6. For more on this Lamar, see Ashley Steenson, "A War of Ideas: L.Q.C. Lamar and American Political Thought" (MA thesis, University of Mississippi, 2020).

7. Lamar, *The Life*, 38–39; Winkle III, "Lamar," 570.

8. Lamar, *The Life*, 41, 47; Winkle III, "Lamar," 570.

William Kimbrough Pendleton

Owing in large part to his exhaustive (and likely exhausting) work in compiling the civil law volume of Georgia's revised state code, Joseph was appointed to the state Supreme Court in 1903.[9] Yet it was a chance encounter, rather than his accomplishments, which put him on a path to the highest Court in the land. A golf enthusiast, Joseph played a round with the recently elected president, William Howard Taft, when the latter visited Augusta in late 1908 or early 1909.[10] The Georgia jurist impressed his executive counterpart, and after William Henry Moody retired

9. Winkle III, "Lamar," 570.

10. William Pruden, "Joseph Rucker Lamar," *New Georgia Encyclopedia*, https://www.georgiaencyclopedia.org/articles/government-politics/ joseph-rucker-lamar-1857-1916/, places the golf outing in late 1908, whereas Winkle III, "Lamar," 570, puts it in 1909.

in 1910, Lamar was nominated to the Court later that year and ultimately took his seat on January 3, 1911.[11]

Two of Lamar's three most notable opinions were issued in his first year on the Court; both support the observation of the *Oxford Companion to the Supreme Court of the United States* that "His noteworthy opinions were those that expanded administrative discretion for executive officials."[12] In *Gompers v. Buck Stove and Range Co.*, Lamar spoke for a unanimous Court to affirm the use of injunctions to end boycotts; later that same year, in *United States v. Grimaud*, Lamar's majority opinion upheld the Forest Reserve Act of 1891 and gave administrators wide leeway in their implementation of the law.[13]

Lamar's most significant contribution as a Justice, however, took him far from the Court's chambers. Lamar was a childhood friend of Woodrow Wilson, who was elected to the presidency in 1912. Despite the partisan differences between Wilson and his predecessor Taft, who had appointed Lamar following their fateful golf outing, Wilson tapped Lamar to serve on a committee representing American interests at the ABC (Argentina, Brazil, Chile) Conference. According to one account, Mexican

> military forces [had been] clashing with civilian officials.
> U.S. intervention efforts, aimed at supporting Mexico's
> democratically elected government, were resisted by the
> Mexican military and left the two nations on the brink
> of war.

---

11. Pruden, "Joseph Rucker Lamar."
12. Winkle III, "Lamar," 570.
13. *Gompers v. Buck Stove and Range Co.*, 221 U.S. 418 (1911); *United States v. Grimaud*, 220 U.S. 506 (1911).

Unfortunately, Lamar's diplomatic service, successful though it was in reducing tensions between the countries, left him exhausted and in flagging health to begin 1915.[14]

1915 was also the year in which a second member of the Disciples of Christ, James Clark McReynolds, was appointed to the Supreme Court. McReynolds grew up in Elkton, Kentucky, where his father was a prominent surgeon and planter.[15]

Justice James Clark McReynolds

Like Lamar, McReynolds was pushed hard by a demanding father. He graduated as valedictorian of Vanderbilt University in 1882 and then from the law school of the University of Virginia in 1884.[16] The young lawyer

14. Pruden, "Joseph Rucker Lamar."

15. Ed Young, "James Clark McReynolds," *Tennessee Encyclopedia*, https://tennesseeencyclopedia.net/entries/james-clark-mcreynolds/.

16. John M. Scheb II, "McReynolds, James Clark," in James W. Ely and Joel B. Grossman, eds., *The Oxford Companion to the Supreme Court of the United States* (New York: Oxford University Press, 2005), 629.

quickly made a name for himself on the Nashville legal scene and was rewarded for his efforts with a law professorship at Vanderbilt in 1900. McReynolds also tested the political waters in 1886, running as a "Gold Democrat" for a congressional seat. He did not win the election, but his campaign drew a significant amount of Republican support, and in 1903, McReynolds was called on by Theodore Roosevelt to serve as assistant attorney general. After his service concluded, McReynolds moved to New York City, once again making waves in the legal world.[17]

McReynolds returned to the public sphere in 1913 when Woodrow Wilson brought him into his cabinet as attorney general.[18] A bit of buyer's remorse on Wilson's part and a timely vacancy on the Supreme Court led the president to nominate McReynolds to the judicial opening just one year later. "McReynolds was eminently qualified to be attorney general," his entry in the *Tennessee Encyclopedia* reads,

> but his violent temper and abrasive personality soon began to create problems for the president. When his fellow Tennessean, Justice [Horace Harmon] Lurton, died in 1914, Wilson seized the opportunity to solve two problems at once by appointing McReynolds to the U.S. Supreme Court.[19]

(The significant problems McReynolds would cause for the following Democratic president, Franklin Delano Roosevelt, were not yet apparent.)

---

17. Scheb II, "McReynolds," 630.
18. Scheb II, "McReynolds," 630.
19. Young, "James Clark McReynolds."

McReynolds's trademark writing style was evident from the start, as shown in his first opinion, *Hopkins v. Hebard*.[20] McReynolds biographer James E. Bond observes that "McReynolds's maiden opinion is remarkable only because it reflects certain peculiar characteristics that typified nearly all his 503 opinions for the Court and mirrored his character as well."[21] The opinion was short, citing and discussing only four authorities and keeping the language plain and unadorned. Yet while some readers might have wished for more explanation from McReynolds in this and his other opinions, Bond continues, "Such abbreviated opinions probably did not trouble his colleagues in his early years on the Court because, with the exception of Holmes and later Brandeis and Clarke, they generally shared McReynolds's views."[22]

The brief professional relationship between Lamar and McReynolds does not seem to have been an overly close one, but the Justices' judicial philosophies and approaches to writing had much in common. Clarinda Pendleton Lamar, Joseph's wife and biographer, noted that his 1915 opinion in *Wadley Southern R.Y. v. Georgia*[23] was, like McReynolds's in *Hopkins v. Hebard*, representative of Lamar's writing style, especially in his attempt to decide the case as a matter of right and wrong rather than based on technicalities.

Lamar's 1915 opinion in *United States v. Midwest Oil Co.*[24] was among his most significant and, like the *Gompers*

---

20. *Hopkins v. Hebard*, 235 U.S. 287 (1914).
21. James E. Bond, *I Dissent: The Legacy of Chief Justice James Clark McReynolds* (Fairfax, VA: George Mason University Press, 1992), 57.
22. Bond, *I Dissent*, 62.
23. U.S. Reports: Wadley Southern R.Y. v. Georgia, 235 U.S. 651 (1915).
24. United States v. Midwest Oil Co., 236 U.S. 459 (1915).

and *Grimaud* opinions noted above, served to expand executive discretion and power. McReynolds did not take part in that decision or in a handful of Lamar's other opinions from their shared time on the Court,[25] but in the remainder, he offered no dissent. Neither did Lamar dissent from any of McReynolds's opinions in that span. Furthermore, the one instance in which one of the Disciples Justices mentioned the other directly was a favorable one; McReynolds approvingly cited Lamar's earlier work in *Loomis v. Lehigh Valley R.R.*

> Speaking through Mr. Justice Lamar in *Mitchell Coal Co. v. Penna. R. R., supra*, we said (p. 255): The courts have not been given jurisdiction to fix rates or practices in direct proceedings, nor can they do so collaterally during the progress of a lawsuit when the action is based on the claim that unreasonable allowances have been paid. If the decision of such questions was committed to different courts with different juries the results would not only vary in degree, but might often be opposite in character-- to the destruction of the uniformity in rate and practice which was the cardinal object of the statute.[26]

The brief window during which the Disciples of Christ were doubly represented on the Supreme Court closed when, in September 1915, Joseph Rucker Lamar suffered a paralytic stroke and was unable to begin the new term.

---

25. These include Henry v. Henkel, 235 U.S. 219 (1914); United States v. Nixon, 235 U.S. 231 (1914); United States v. Salen, 235 U.S. 237 (1914); United States v. Sherman, 237 U.S. 146 (1915); Louis. & Nash. R.R. v. United States, 238 U.S. 1 (1915); and United States v. Del., Lack., & West R.R., 238 U.S. 516 (1915).

26. Loomis v. Lehigh Valley R. R., 240 U.S. 43, 49 (1916).

Already in declining health before the stroke, Lamar lingered for a few months but passed away at his home in Washington on January 2, 1916. His body was taken back to Augusta, Georgia, two days later and was buried on the 5th.[27] So ended a stay on the Court, which was characterized by brevity and affability.

Neither of these characteristics could be accurately applied to the tenure of the Court's other Disciple. James E. Bond is likely correct when he writes that

> Had McReynolds resigned from the bench in the early twenties or retired at the end of that decade, his name would barely survive. He would be recalled if at all as one of a dozen or so competent but undistinguished Justices who labored with their more brilliant brethren ... to maintain the generally conservative mien of the Court ....[28]

But McReynolds stayed on until 1945.

In 1925, McReynolds did offer a particularly notable opinion in the case of *Pierce v. Society of Sisters*, in which the Court struck down a state-level law mandating children's attendance at public schools.[29] This was one of several McReynolds-authored opinions written in defense of individual civil liberties.[30] Yet the Justice was far better

---

27. Pruden, "Joseph Rucker Lamar"; Lamar, *The Life*, 276–280.

28. Bond, *I Dissent*, 135. Put simply, if McReynolds's tenure had been as short as Lamar's, he would have been remembered (or forgotten) like Lamar.

29. Pierce v. Society of Sisters, 268 U.S. 510 (1925).

30. Young, "James Clark McReynolds." Law professor Todd C. Peppers places *Meyer v. Nebraska* in this category, writing that "In the *Meyer* case, McReynolds drafted an opinion which overturned a Nebraska law outlawing the teaching of German in public schools; in *Pierce*, McReynolds—writing for a unanimous court—found that a law requiring

known for being difficult to work with. A major component of this trouble was McReynolds's anti-Semitism; he was anything but collegial towards colleague Benjamin Cardozo and "at one time ... actually left the conference room whenever [Louis] Brandeis spoke. The two Justices apparently were never on speaking terms" despite having been appointed by the same president.[31]

In terms of his judicial philosophy, McReynolds found himself numbered, along with George Sutherland, Willis Van Devanter, and Pierce Butler, among the "Four Horsemen" or "Battalion of Death" who opposed Roosevelt's New Deal at every turn.[32] Especially in the years from 1935 through 1937, these four voted together consistently, often joined by a more moderate member of the Court, to stymie various pieces of New Deal legislation. Yet the famous "switch in time that saved nine"—the movement of the Court's moderates to a less antagonistic stance—combined with personnel changes to leave McReynolds on the losing side of the argument. Van Devanter and Sutherland retired in 1938, and Butler followed in 1940.[33] Of the Horsemen, only McReynolds remained, and while his opinions remained as anti-New Deal as ever, he found himself out of

children to attend public schools violated their parents' liberty interests in deciding how their children would be educated. Modern courts have drawn upon McReynolds' reasoning in these cases, including cases involving reproductive freedom." See Todd C. Peppers, "Cancelling Justice? The Case of James Clark McReynolds," *Richmond Public Interest Law Review* 24, no. 2 (2021): 68–69.

31. Tony Freyer, *Hugo L. Black and the Dilemma of American Liberalism* (Glenview, IL: Scott, Foresman/Little, Brown Higher Education, 1990), 74.

32. David M. Kennedy, *Freedom from Fear: The American People in Depression and War, 1929–1945* (New York: Oxford University Press, 1999), 263, 326.

33. Freyer, *Hugo L. Black*, 81; Kennedy, *Freedom from Fear*, 336.

step with his colleagues and unable to stop the broader changes he feared.[34]

Even though he had promised to remain on the bench to oppose FDR, McReynolds wound up resigning in 1945.[35] Five years later, the Justice contracted bronchial pneumonia, died, and was buried in his hometown of Elkton, Kentucky. Only after his death was it revealed that McReynolds had been financially supporting thirty-three English refugees who had been impacted by German bombing in 1941.[36]

The Lamar-McReynolds pairing could not and should not be considered one of the all-time great judicial alliances; one Justice is mostly forgotten, and to the extent that the other is remembered, it is mostly negatively.[37] Still, the two men help illustrate the increased prominence of the Stone-Campbell Movement, and of the Disciples of Christ more specifically, on the national political stage. As the son of J.S. Lamar and the son-in-law of W.K. Pendleton, J.R. Lamar was practically Stone-Campbell royalty; he served as a trustee for his father's congregation in Augusta, Georgia, and would even speak there on occasion.[38] McReynolds's father was just as devoted to the movement as Lamar's (he

---

34. For more, see John W. Compton, *The Evangelical Origins of the Living Constitution* (Cambridge, MA: Harvard University Press, 2014), 167–172. In a particularly telling example, Compton observes on 172, "That [Butler and McReynolds] declined to offer any theoretical justification whatsoever for allowing Congress to impinge upon the local sphere of 'morals' while simultaneously barring it from the local sphere of 'production' suggested that even the remaining Horsemen were aware that the conceptual foundations of dual federalism were crumbling."

35. Kennedy, *Freedom from Fear*, 336.

36. Young, "James Clark McReynolds."

37. Bond does not include any cases from the period in which Lamar and McReynolds overlapped in the appendices to *I Dissent*.

38. Lamar, *The Life*, 60.

single-handedly paid the salary of the full-time minister of the Elkton, Kentucky, congregation for a period), and the Justice included the National City Christian Church in Washington, DC, in his will.[39]

National City Christian Church

Perhaps their brief window of shared responsibility can serve as a jumping-off point for further exploration of the political and legal impacts of the Stone-Campbell Movement, and of the connections between Justices of "like precious faith."

39. Bond, *I Dissent*, 5, 136 n5.

Chapter 7

The Golden Rule or the Gospel of Wealth?

J.R. McWane and the Disciples of Christ

ALABAMANS TODAY LIKELY RECOGNIZE THE "MCWANE" family name from one of two Birmingham-area fixtures: McWane, Inc., a privately held manufacturing firm which has generated significant controversy for its health and safety record; or the McWane Science Center,

McWane Science Center

a much beloved museum, archive, and IMAX theater. Despite the metaphorical distance between these two Central Alabama institutions, each reflects an important aspect of family patriarch James Ransom (J.R.) McWane's economic philosophy.

James Ransom McWane

J.R. broke with his previous employer, ACIPCO, and founded his own company because he sharply disagreed with ACIPCO founder John Eagan's "Golden Rule" business practices; yet J.R. was a devout member, lay minister, and financial booster of First Christian Church of Birmingham and a leading figure within many national Disciples of Christ organizations. This chapter explores J.R.'s apparent preference for Andrew Carnegie's "Gospel of Wealth" over Eagan's "Golden Rule" and the impacts his adherence to Carnegie's short treatise, with its twin emphases on profit and philanthropy, had for the Disciples of Christ in Birmingham and beyond.

The American Cast Iron Pipe Company, founded by John Eagan in 1905, has long been seen as a desirable employer in Alabama's industrial capital of Birmingham. The foundry has been a remarkably safe place to work and significantly less harmful to the environment, at least compared to its peers. Especially attractive to many is the plant's collective ownership model, under which workers maintain a financial interest in the company even after they retire. Such concern for the physical and financial well-being of plant workers has long been fixed at the top of the organizational chart. Most notably, in the final few years prior to his 1924 death, Eagan repurchased all the outstanding shares of his company and willed them to his employees as part of his broader "Golden Rule" approach to business management,[1] which also placed four representatives of the company's workforce on its board of operatives. "That year," according to one account, "employees responded to Eagan's reorganization with record-breaking production numbers."[2]

Although these changes were almost universally praised at the time, one high-ranking employee—the company's president, James Ransom (J.R.) McWane—pushed back hard against them. Accounts vary somewhat as to whether McWane was forced out or left in protest, but in any event, he was overruled by Eagan and out of a job by 1921. The promising young executive had originally been poached from the nearby Birmingham Steel and Iron Company and installed as ACIPCO's vice president in 1908, rising to the company's presidency in 1915. Particularly noteworthy was his oversight and financing of the Vulcan statue, originally created for the World's Fair in 1904 but later relocated from St. Louis to Birmingham.[3]

So, who was James Ransom McWane? Was he some sort of Robert Owen-style tycoon and critic of the Christian faith? Hardly. Around the same time that he established his namesake company, McWane was serving on the board of

---

1. "Two Companies, Two Visions," *Frontline*, https://www.pbs.org/wgbh/pages/frontline/shows/workplace/mcwane/two.html.

2. Scotty Kirkland, "Retrospect: ACIPCO President John J. Eagan applied 'Golden Rule' to industry," *Business Alabama*, September 28, 2023, https://businessalabama.com/retrospect-acipco-president-john-j-eagan-applies-golden-rule-to-industry/.

3. "Two Companies, Two Visions."

what is now Berry College in Georgia,[4] a member and then vice president of the Alabama State Board of the Disciples of Christ, the vice president of the Disciples' state convention, the primus inter pares of the building committee for First Christian Church of Birmingham, a trustee for the proposed "University School of Religion" in nearby Tuscaloosa,[5] and a booster of the Disciples' Pension Fund and the United Christian Missionary Society.[6]

As committed to the Disciples of Christ in doctrine and dollars as a person could be, why did McWane so strongly oppose the institution of Eagan's "Golden Rule" capitalism at ACIPCO that he either quit in protest or was forced out? Information on J.R. and later generations of the McWane family remains hard to come by; the family and company (one of the largest privately held firms in the country) remain particularly tight-lipped today. But based on his interest in maximizing profits at all costs and his equal dedication to giving away significant amounts of those profits, it seems likely that McWane had imbibed not only the restorationist theology of Disciples leader Alexander Campbell but also the "Gospel of Wealth" associated most famously with the Scottish-American titan of industry Andrew Carnegie. Carnegie's philosophy has become part of the McWane inheritance, too. Subsequent generations of the family have established the treasured McWane Science

---

4. "Commencement Exercises at Berry School to Begin April 29 and Close May 2," *Rome Tribune-Herald*, April 20, 1916.

5. For more on this educational effort, see John Young, "Disciples of Christ and The University of Alabama School that Wasn't," *Alabama Review* 75.3 (July 2022): 199–224.

6. George H. Watson and Mildred B. Watson, *History of the Christian Churches in the Alabama Area* (St. Louis: The Bethany Press, 1965), 268–269.

Center and contributed generously to efforts as varied as the Vulcan Fund, the Sloss Furnaces Foundation, and the Children's Hospital of Alabama,[7] all while the company, according to David Barstow and Lowell Bergman in the *New York Times*, remained "one of the most dangerous businesses in America."[8]

James Ransom McWane was born on August 15, 1869, in Wytheville, Virginia, and graduated from the Disciples' flagship Bethany College in neighboring West Virginia in 1891. In 1904, J.R. moved his family, including his son William, born in 1898, to the boomtown of Birmingham so that he could take on the presidency of the Birmingham Steel and Iron Company. McWane almost immediately began oversight of the construction of the famous Vulcan statue for that year's World's Fair. Although he was not compensated for his services—which, in fact, nearly led to the family's financial ruin—McWane was clearly making a name for himself; in 1908, ACIPCO hired him away to serve as its vice president, and McWane reached the presidency of the company in 1915. A highly favorable profile of J.R. appeared in the November 1920 issue of *System*, which claimed that

> Perhaps no man has introduced a greater number of revolutionizing innovations into the pipe-making business than McWane .... But it is not alone in mechanical ingenuity that McWane excels. His ingenious and compre-

7. "William McWane," Alabama Business Hall of Fame, https://abhof. culverhouse.ua.edu/member/william-mcwane/; "C. Phillip McWane," Alabama Business Hall of Fame, https://abhof.culverhouse.ua.edu/ member/c-phillip-mcwane/.
8. Daniel Barstow and Lowell Bergman, "A Family's Fortune, a Legacy of Blood and Tears," *New York Times*, January 9, 2003.

hensive welfare work is not alone a 'good policy' idea, but is also an expression of his sincere interest in human beings.[9]

It was in this era that McWane grew so closely involved with First Christian Church of Birmingham, a congregation of the Disciples of Christ. This band of Christians had originally been brought together in 1874 by Colonel J.J. Jolly soon after his arrival in town; yet when his family moved on from Birmingham four years later, the small gathering, which had been meeting in various rental spaces, faded out. In the winter of 1885, however, a group of women began organizing a Sunday School meeting, which helped spur the congregation's resurrection. Three years later, the church built its first wooden structure, affectionately known as the "Tabernacle," and by 1903 or 1904, had moved into a red brick building at the corner of 5th Avenue North and 21st Street. In 1924, the developer of the Redmont Hotel purchased the facility from the congregation, which moved into a new building two blocks north. J.R. McWane helped raise the funds for this structure, and his younger brother, A.T., would play a similarly crucial role when the church eventually raised a new sanctuary next door. First Christian Church would stay in this downtown location until 1981 when it relocated to Valleydale Road in Shelby County.[10]

---

9. A.F. Harlow, "James R. McWane: Who finds it profitable to study his equipment and to study his men," *System*, November 1920.
10. Kate G. Dyleski, "First Christian Church, Sunday Morning Worship: All Are Welcome as God Has Welcomed Us," *Magic City Religion: Observations on Religion in Birmingham, Alabama, by Samford University Religious Studies Students*, May 20, 2021, https://magiccityreligion.org/2021/05/20/first-christian-church-birmingham-disciples-of-christ-sunday-morning-worship/; "First Christian Church," Bhamwiki, https://www.bhamwiki.com/w/First_Christian_Church; William O. Holcombe,

Of course, this kind of charitable and religious involvement (J.R. was even an ordained minister!) did not lead McWane to support John Eagan's "Golden Rule" philosophy at ACIPCO. Rather, McWane's actions and the few glimpses we can get into his mindset fit squarely within the framework established in Andrew Carnegie's article "Wealth," more commonly known as the "Gospel of Wealth." Carnegie first published "Wealth" in 1889, and in it, according to biographer Harold C. Livesay, he

> elaborated on his earlier reflections that he had a personal responsibility to "spend the surplus... for benevolent purposes." In it Carnegie remarked publicly (as he had already told Gladstone privately) that a man who died rich died disgraced. The rich man had a duty to dispose of his wealth by supporting useful institutions, of which he listed seven: universities, libraries, hospitals, parks, meeting and concert halls, swimming pools, and church buildings. In these benefactions the rich fulfilled the only function that justified their existence—accumulating wealth for the uplift of the general populace.[11]

Carnegie went even further than this, arguing that while capitalism was the best, or at least the least bad, of competing economic systems, one of its chief downsides was the creation of great fortunes such as his own; this was a bug, not a feature, of the system. In turn, class conflict would erupt and lead to disunity (and perhaps worse) along

Claradel Holcombe, and Jimmy Langley, *First Christian Church Birmingham: 150 Years: A History* (2024).

11. Harold C. Livesay, *Andrew Carnegie and the Rise of Big Business*, 2nd ed. (New York: Longman, 2000), 141–142.

economic lines. Encouraging the truly wealthy to spend their money on behalf of society, preferably during their lifetimes, was Carnegie's goal; but he was no Pollyanna about what might work best to motivate this change in behavior.

> Nor need it be feared that this policy would sap the root of enterprise and render men less anxious to accumulate, for to the class whose ambition it is to leave great fortunes and be talked about after their death, it will attract even more attention, and, indeed, be a somewhat nobler ambition to have enormous sums paid over to the state from their fortunes.[12]

Two other newspaper reports give some insight into the mind of McWane. A 1915 article in the *Dubuque Telegraph-Herald* pointed to the enthusiasm of big business for the YMCA, especially in large cities across the nation. J.R. was, at the time, still vice president of ACIPCO, which had spent $45,000 establishing a YMCA branch for its employees' use. One imagines that this may have been Eagan's doing, but McWane also spoke positively of it in explicitly financial terms: "The money invested in the Y.M.C.A. pays better than the same amount of money invested in any other building in our plant."[13] The 1920 *Source* profile of J.R. also makes mention of "A big Y.M.C.A. building ... among the town's numerous public buildings."[14] McWane's

---

12. Andrew Carnegie, "The Gospel of Wealth," 6, https://media.carnegie. org/filer_public/ab/c9/abc9fb4b-dc86-4ce8-ae31-a983b9a326ed/ccny_es say_1889_thegospelofwealth.pdf.

13. "Plans for Y.M.C.A. Building Underway," *Dubuque Telegraph-Herald*, April 11, 1915.

14. Harlow, "James R. McWane."

personal faith also features heavily in that report, especially its impact on the workforce—mostly Black—of ACIPCO. According to the paper:

> The majority of the employees of the company are negroes, and negroes form a peculiar and interesting problem for the employer of labor. They must be handled in a different manner from white men. McWane is credited with understanding the Southern negro about as well as, perhaps better than, any other employer in the country. He pays consider attention to the religious side of his work—religion makes a strong appeal to the negro. And McWane deals with him sincerely in this respect—for he himself is a deeply religious man.
>
> His negro employees looking up to him not only as the big boss but as a moral leader, a character worthy of emulation, and the source of all knowledge.[15]

Still, even here, the usefulness of religion is cast in financial terms, with its ability to boost morale and, presumably, productivity among the company's mostly Black laborers.

Whether J.R. McWane read Andrew Carnegie's work or simply absorbed its precepts in some other capacity, the company he established in the 1920s would be operated on that basis. The new business grew rapidly in its early years, with the establishment of a second facility, the Pacific States Cast Iron Pipe Company, located in Provo, Utah, in 1926. J.R. continued to be seen as a wunderkind of his industry, addressing the Joint Meeting of the Plant Management and Operators and the Fire Protection Divisions at the Buffalo,

---

15. Harlow, "James R. McWane."

New York, meeting of the American Water Works Association in June 1925. His paper, "Standard Lengths of Cast Iron Pipe Cast Horizontally," was later published in the organization's journal.[16]

By 1929, McWane's finances were secure enough that he was able to relocate his family to a substantial Mountain Brook estate. But just four years later, on June 24, 1933, while traveling in Chicago on business, J.R. experienced a heart attack and died suddenly. His son, William, replaced him as president of McWane, followed by his son, also named James R. McWane, in 1971, and then by his son, C. Phillip McWane, who began serving on the company's board in 1986. These and subsequent years have brought the family and company visibility, or scrutiny, along two tracks: positive recognition for the company's financial success and family's charitable giving, and decidedly negative portrayals in a pair of *Frontline* documentaries and a scathing expose in the *New York Times*. Both are part and parcel of the J.R. McWane legacy.

---

16. J.R. McWane, "Standard Lengths of Cast Iron Pipe Cast Horizontally," *Journal AWWA* 16.5 (November 1926): 620–624.

Chapter 8

"He's human even if he is a Campbellite"

T.S. Stribling and the Stone-Campbell Movement

AFTER A VERY BRIEF foray into law school in the fall of 2012, I started taking graduate-level coursework in history in the spring of 2013, fully entering the master's program at the University of Alabama in the fall of that year. I soon needed to pick out a topic for the following spring's research seminar—something I was interested in, something that had a manageable source base, something on which I could make a small but meaningful scholarly contribution. I narrowed my choices down to two. I would research and write on the preacher and teacher T.B. Larimore's attempt to start a Christian college and colony in Gainesville, Florida, during the 1910s; or I would focus on the chilly reception which Pulitzer-winning novelist T.S. Stribling received from the Shoals area, a lightly fictionalized version of which he used as the setting for his Vaiden trilogy. Both men had important ties to my hometown of Florence, they were representative of broader trends in southern history (especially important given the professors who would be leading the seminar), and the projects were just the right size for a semester's worth of work.

I dithered on deciding until my birthday, when my girl-friend, now wife, surprised me with a copy of *Life, Letters, and Sermons of T.B. Larimore.* Whether coincidental or providential, I decided to focus on the Larimore project. This proved to be a good decision, leading to my first peer-reviewed article[1] and then eventually to a professional research agenda devoted primarily to the history of the Stone-Campbell Movement.

The decision to go down the Larimore path certainly turned out well over the long run, but I have always wondered how things might have proceeded if I had taken on the Stribling project instead. Would I have still ended up working on Restoration Movement history? It's possible. After all, Stribling had some interesting and important ties to the movement—more on that later.

T.S. Stribling was born in the Wayne County, Tennessee, community of Clifton in 1881, the same year that Disciples of Christ member James A. Garfield reached the White House.[2]

---

1. John Young, "Dixieland's Demise: T.B. Larimore's Dixieland College and the Tenuous Position of Christian Colleges within the Churches of Christ," *Restoration Quarterly* 58.3 (2016): 143–159.

2. Much of the biographical information in this section comes from Jefferson T. Spurlock, "T.S. Stribling," *Encyclopedia of Alabama,* https://encyclopediaofalabama.org/article/t-s-stribling/.

T.S. Stribling

Stribling's father, Christopher Columbus Stribling, was what he described as "a 'modified atheist' who believed in God but not the deity of Christ," whereas his mother, Amelia Waits Stribling, was "a 'modified churchist' who believed in churches but not in ministers."[3] This skepticism towards organized religion powerfully influenced young Stribling, who, at his father's urging, pursued education at Florence Normal School (now the University of North Alabama)[4] and then the law school of the University of Alabama. Stribling soon found work in local law offices, including that of Alabama governor Emmet O'Neal, but his

---

3.　Kenneth W. Vickers, *T.S. Stribling: A Life of the Tennessee Novelist* (Knoxville, TN: University of Tennessee Press, 2004), 20–21.

4.　According to "The Normal College—Interesting Commencement Exercises" in the *Florence Times* of June 5, 1903, Stribling won the "Essayist's medal" and was listed as an advanced graduate of the school.

passion was for writing, and he instead made his way to Nashville and the editorial department of the *Taylor-Trotwood Magazine*.[5] He also found time to write Sunday School materials as a side job, an admittedly unusual line of work for a religious skeptic:

> I can say this about Sunday school stories, and I am sure I have written ten thousand, they allow a far wider latitude of thought and philosophy than any one dreams of who has not followed that market.[6]

Of course, Stribling had a connection to organized religion at one point in his life. He regularly stayed at the Lauderdale County home of his uncle Lee and aunt Etta Waits. The couple was part of the congregation at Gravelly Springs, and Stribling wrote at length about his visits to the church. While he semi-jokingly attributed his newfound faith to the influence of his aunt's cooking ("Under the influence of the cobblers, all my Cliftonian arguments against religion not only were hushed, they absolutely disappeared from my mind"),[7] he wrote with a mixture of sincere interest and curiosity toward the church's practices. "The Campbellites prided themselves on their pure logic, their adherence to reason, and their undemonstrativeness." Stribling similarly imagined the preacher

---

5. "News Items of Interest," *Florence Times*, November 13, 1908.
6. Quoted in Randy K. Cross, introduction to T.S. Stribling, *The Forge: An Epic Novel of the War-Torn South* (New York: Doubleday, Doran & Company, 1931; Tuscaloosa, AL: University of Alabama Press, 1985), vi.
7. T.S. Stribling, *Laughing Stock: The Posthumous Autobiography*, eds. Randy K. Cross and John T. McMillan (Memphis, TN: St. Luke's Press, 1982), 72.

up in his pulpit, leafing here and there through his Bible, reading the exact chapter and verse which were his proofs, and giving his congregation the references so they could go home and read them too, and make sure there was no logical flaw in God's contract with sinners.[8]

Stribling read scripture through a decidedly more mystical lens, however, and abandoned his churchgoing altogether when he returned to Clifton.[9]

The Waitses were not Stribling's only family connection to the Restoration Movement, though. His mule trader cousin John Y. Parker left an endowment in his will to keep a preacher working in Wayne County, Tennessee.[10] Another cousin, J.H. Stribling of Lawrence County, Tennessee, was converted through the preaching of T.B. Larimore after the untimely death of his young daughter Gladys.[11] J.H. Stribling maintained a correspondence with T.B. Larimore after his conversion, and he was a supporter of R.H. Boll, who eulogized him in the pages of his journal, the *Word and Work*.[12]

These and perhaps other points of connection between T.S. Stribling and the Restoration Movement impacted his writing in important ways. In August 1905, Stribling was tapped to write an obituary for Florence-area minister Persia Hiram (P.H.) Hooten, a piece which was published

---

8. Stribling, *Laughing Stock*, 72–73.
9. Stribling, *Laughing Stock*, 74–75.
10. Stribling, *Laughing Stock*, 68.
11. Harliana Burns, "From Sworn Enemies to Nazi Neighbors to Found Family: The Impact of a World War II German POW Camp on a Rural Tennessee Community and the POWs Who Lived There" (MA thesis, Middle Tennessee State University, 2021), 27, 33.
12. Included at "James Henry Stribling, 1863–1951," https://www.therestorationmovement.com/_states/tennessee/stribling.htm.

in the *Gospel Advocate*. Hooten had been serving, most recently, as the minister of what is now Wood Avenue Church of Christ in downtown Florence.[13] Stribling closed his remembrance of Hooten with the following thoughts:

> Little need be said of our brother's character. No words of ours could make stronger or deeper the gentle, lasting love and respect of his many friends; neither could we hope to make strangers feel the charm of his person, his genial bearing, his delicate courtesy, his manly love of right and truth, his contempt of what was wrong.... Could there be any higher, nobler, truer commentary on human character, when delirium, which racks our body and brings out the very worst in us, produced in him only hallowed thoughts and kindly blessings—the unconscious utterance of a pure and stainless soul?[14]

Interactions with the Restoration Movement heritage also colored the North Alabama of Stribling's most famous and influential work, the Vaiden trilogy. These three books —*The Forge*, published in 1930, *The Store*, in 1932, and *The Unfinished Cathedral*, in 1934—are filled with discussions of religious beliefs, individuals, and institutions. In fact, Anne French Dalke, writing in the *Southern Literary Journal*, argues that "Stribling's main concern, this the point

---

13. Mary Nell King and Hiawatha Walker, *A History of the Church of Christ at Poplar Street and Wood Avenue, Florence, Alabama, 1886–1986* (Florence, AL: Country Lane Printing, 1986), 121.

14. T.S. Stribling, "Persia Hiram Hooten," *Gospel Advocate*, August 3, 1905. For more, see Christopher R. Cotten, "'A Relentless Warfare Against the Inventions and Devices of Man': John T. Lewis and the Churches of Christ in Birmingham, Alabama, 1907–1967" (MDiv thesis, Lipscomb University, 2013), 9 n9.

to which all three novels are heading [is] the loss, the perversion, of the religious vitality of the South."[15] Jimmie Vaiden, the patriarch of the family whose story anchors the trilogy,

> is a hard-shell Baptist whose best friend is a Methodist circuit rider primarily because Jimmy [sic] could get into good arguments with a Methodist. Jimmy didn't like the Campbellite preacher because Jimmy's simple mind couldn't find enough difference between hard-shell doctrine and Campbellism to argue about.[16]

(The quotation from which this chapter takes its title comes directly from Jimmie, who is criticizing the preacher.) After Jimmie's death at the end of *The Forge*, his son, Miltiades, becomes the focal point of the next two books. In *The Store*, he tells his nephew Jerry Catlin that

> we Vaidens are an old and a naturally religious family. Your grandfather was a Hard-shell Baptist. Your great-grandfather, Simeon Vaiden, who lived in South Carolina, was a shouting Methodist who got converted under John Wesley himself. I'm a Christian; people call me a Campbellite. Now, I didn't really expect you to become a Campbellite. I sort of thought the new generation would take up its own church just as we Vaidens always have done.[17]

15. Anne French Dalke, "'Love ought to be like religion, Brother Milt': An Examination of the Civil War and Reconstruction Trilogy of T.S. Stribling," *Southern Literary Journal* 14.1 (Fall 1981): 29–30.

16. Walter L. Fertig, "Maurice Thompson's Primitive Baptist Heritage," *Indiana Magazine of History* 64.1 (March 1968): 7.

17. T.S. Stribling, *The Store: A Stirring Novel of the Post-Reconstruction*

Earlier in that same novel, Jerry makes an impromptu visit to Florence's "Campbellite church," and his perception of it sounds remarkably like Stribling's characterization of the Gravelly Springs congregation. The preacher's sermon "was a precise geometrical analysis of the will of God, and if his congregation lost a single minor premise his whole demonstration would be thrown away." The goal of the sermon was to bring the hearers to heaven, "an Oriental Jewish city built of gold and elaborately decorated with jewels, which was the exact antithesis of the church in which they sat."[18] The song leader had to periodically hum middle C during the sermon to keep the pitch ready for the invitation, and the only musical flourish to be heard besides the human voice came from the tolling of the church's bell at the appointed hour.[19]

T.S. Stribling may seem an odd choice of subject for a chapter in this book, admittedly, but his importance to the history of the Shoals area, southern literature, and, as it turns out, the Stone-Campbell Movement makes him a fitting selection all the same.

South (New York: Doubleday, Doran & Company, 1932; Tuscaloosa, AL: University of Alabama Press, 1985), 136.

18. Stribling, *The Store*, 55–56.

19. Stribling, *The Store*, 56, 185.

Chapter 9

Father, Son, and Spirit(s)

The Curious Case of H.W.B. Myrick

CHURCH HISTORY often offers the researcher tantalizing tidbits that they simply can't chase down at the time. Sometimes the tangent would take the author too far from the subject at hand; sometimes a deadline looms. But occasionally they can double back. Such was the case for me when, back in the spring of 2014, I conducted the bulk of my research on T.B. Larimore's proposed "Dixieland" Christian college and colony during a graduate-level research seminar at the University of Alabama.[1]

---

1. This research was published as John Young, "Dixieland's Demise: T.B. Larimore's Dixieland College and the Tenuous Position of Christian Colleges within the Churches of Christ," *Restoration Quarterly* 58.3 (2016): 143–159.

T. B. Larimore

Given that the seminar was, in fact, a class, there were grades, and there were deadlines.

Yet one of the professors leading the seminar suggested to me that I check out a *Florida Historical Quarterly* article on the Spiritualist community at Cassadaga, which would provide some historical context from beyond the bounds of the Stone-Campbell Movement.[2] The piece, one of several scholarly works on Cassadaga, was, in fact, an interesting entry point into the literature on intentional religious communities in the Sunshine State. (This is a surprisingly large category, as evidenced by the existence of an entire volume devoted to the subject.)[3] I also came to realize over time that other kinds of Florida-based intentional communi-

---

2. John J. Guthrie, Jr., "Seeking the Sweet Spirit of Harmony: Establishing a Spiritualist Community at Cassadaga, Florida, 1893–1933," *Florida Historical Quarterly* 77.1 (1998): 1–38.

3. Nick Wynne and Joe Knetsch, *Utopian Communities of Florida: A History of Hope* (Charleston, SC: The History Press, 2016).

ties—namely, sprawling residential and retirement communities—were having something of a cultural "moment," becoming the subjects of books[4] and documentaries[5] and the settings for popular works of fiction which I happened to encounter along the way.[6]

Still, I was surprised to find in the Cassadaga story an extended discussion of the Reverend H.W.B. Myrick, a former "Campbellite" preacher from Indianapolis who was also a featured speaker at the thirty-fifth anniversary of the Spiritualist community's founding. In the article, Myrick was described as a "well-known [Spiritualist]" and an outspoken evangelist for his newfound religious commitments:

> From his personal experience riding the circuit, Myrick had learned that Christian audiences needed little or no persuading to join the church. In contrast, spreading Spiritualism proved much more difficult.... As he put it, "I did not come from a Christian pulpit into Spiritualism to condemn anybody." Instead, he wanted to retain all the good things in the Bible—the splendor of mercy, the nobility of forgiveness, and the grandeur of self-denial.[7]

Again, I was unable to pursue any inquiry into the mysterious Myrick at the time, but the reference to his

---

4. Andrew D. Blechman, *Leisureville: Adventures in a World Without Children* (New York: Grove Press, 2008).
5. *Some Kind of Heaven*, directed by Lance Oppenheim, produced by Darren Aronofsky (2020; Magnolia Pictures, 2021), Prime Video, https://www.amazon.com/gp/video/detail/B08SQ9W7VR/ref=msx_wn_av.
6. E.L. Konigsburg, *The View from Saturday* (New York: Scholastic, 1996); David Hopen, *The Orchard: A Novel* (New York: HarperCollins, 2020).
7. Guthrie Jr., "Seeking the Sweet Spirit," 35.

"Campbellite" past stayed in my mind. So, when some unrelated readings brought me back to the subject of planned communities in the Stone-Campbell heritage,[8] I decided to take advantage of the opportunity. What I found helped me see that Myrick was an even more interesting figure than I had supposed and that the story of his conversion to Spiritualism was more complex than a simple swapping of faiths.

According to his obituary, Henry Ward Beecher Myrick was born in 1856 in Morgan County, Indiana. His parents moved the family to Missouri when he was twelve, though he traveled often as a young "singing evangelist" during his teens. The congregation at Gentryville, Missouri, where he worshipped, also served as his first, last, and most beloved ministry position.[9] Myrick did preach for churches throughout Missouri, Iowa, Kansas, and Oklahoma during his working years but retired to Gentryville and continued to preach monthly in his old age. A sudden manifestation of an ongoing heart condition took his life in February 1937.[10] (Though hardly the most bizarre incident related to Myrick, the unwinding of his estate, including a two-hundred-acre farm, led to an extended legal battle that was not resolved until it reached the Missouri Supreme Court in 1965.)[11]

---

8. Specifically, Earl Irvin West's brief reference to J.D. Tant's desire to establish a Christian colony in Cuba, a setting explored at much greater length elsewhere in this volume.

9. For more on the early history of the movement in Gentry County, Missouri, see T.P. Haley, *Early Missouri Preachers*, 2 vols. (St. Louis, MO: Christian Publishing Co., 1888; repr. ed. Hester Publications), 509–510. Pagination continues across the two volumes.

10. "Gentry County's Oldest Preacher Dies: Henry Ward Beecher Myrick, of Gentryville, Succumbs—Had a Varied Career," *King City Chronicle*, February 18, 1937.

11. *Prior v. Prior*, 395 S.W.2d 438 (Mo. 1965).

Myrick's obituary emphasizes his service to the church and does not refer directly to any interest in Spiritualism other than a brief reference that "his spirit passed on to the Great Beyond"—hardly a smoking gun—and a short discussion of his work as a traveling lecturer. "As a lecturer," it notes, "he visited every large city from New York to Los Angeles and from the Canadian border to the Gulf of Mexico." Intentionally or otherwise, no indication of the content of Myrick's lectures is given.[12] In fact, the obituary left out several of the most important details about Myrick's lifework, beyond the normal sermons and funerals[13] that occupy a minister's time. H.W.B. penned the lyrics to at least one hymn, known variously as "Far Down the Misty Aisle" or "There Remaineth a Rest," which begins,

> *Far down the misty aisle of time*
> *Beyond the clouds and night*
> *By faith we view a better clime*
> *A land more fair and bright.*[14]

Along with this unacknowledged hymn-writing, Myrick authored at least two short stories for the *New York Weekly*

---

12. "Gentry County's Oldest Preacher Dies."

13. H.W.B. Myrick, obituary for Martha Jane Sampson Yeater, *Ledger*, June 22, 1906, https://www.findagrave.com/memorial/18236538/martha_jane-yeater; "Martin Miller Called by Death: Local Resident Dies At Home After Illness of Asthma and Heart Disease," *Shelbyville Republican*, July 25, 1933, https://www.shelbycountyindiana.org/obituaries/obit_miller.htm; "James J. Evans Died Saturday: Death Claimed Well Known Gentry County Farmer at His Home Near Here Last Saturday Night," *Stanberry Headlight*, September 2, 1937, https://web.pdx.edu/~davide/gene/Evans_James_Johnson.htm.

14. "There remaineth a rest," *Hymnary*, https://hymnary.org/text/far_down_the_misty_aisle.

during the 1880s, "The Bachelors' Club" and "What a Set of Whiskers Did."[15]

Myrick also had more than a passing interest in Spiritualism, of course, and seems to have held these convictions alongside his membership in the Christian Church. Aside from the aforementioned speech at the Cassadaga anniversary gathering, Myrick twice addressed the Iowa meeting of the Mississippi Valley Spiritualists Association in 1920; the title of his first talk, "The Fruits of the Spirit," sounds as if it could reflect either or both of his religious affiliations.[16] Likewise, his essay, "A Peculiar People," which appeared decades later in the *National Spiritualist* but based on the title alone, would not have seemed out of place in a Disciples journal.[17]

Speaking of Disciples periodicals, Myrick made two contributions to the *Christian Quarterly Review* in 1882 and 1883 on the topics of "Inspiration" and "Fore-knowledge."[18] His most significant appearances in movement publications came roughly two decades later, however, when he wound up on the receiving end of criticism from two fellow ministers. The April 3, 1902, *Christian Evangelist* contained a letter from Geo. T. Camp,[19] who took

---

15. H.W.B. Myrick, "The Bachelors' Club," *New York Weekly*, May 25, 1885, https://dimenovels.org/Item/65732/Show; H.W.B. Myrick, "What a Set of Whiskers Did," *New York Weekly*, October 31, 1881, https://dimenovels.org/Item/85407/Show.

16. Materials from *Clinton Advertiser*, August 4, 1920, https://iagenweb.org/clinton/places/clinton/spiritualist.html.

17. H.W.B. Myrick, "A Peculiar People," *National Spiritualist*, September 1978.

18. H.W.B. Myrick, "Inspiration," *Christian Quarterly Review*, October 1882; H.W.B. Myrick, "Fore-knowledge," *Christian Quarterly Review*, April 1883.

19. Geo. T. Camp, "Reply to HWB Myrick," *Christian Evangelist*, April 3, 1902.

exception to Myrick's recent writings as to whether it was necessary to hold a literal interpretation of the Bible's more unusual stories, such as those of Jonah and Balaam when in other contexts those stories might not be taken seriously.[20] It was Myrick's acceptance of the stories as allegories or fables that drew Camp's ire, as well as the attention of H.W. Robertson, who wrote a week later to continue the critique:

> Now, I have not a bit of faith in Sinbad the sailor, hence his stories are discredited at the start. But I have infinite faith in Jesus and he says Jonah was three days and nights in the belly of the fish and since I know he cannot lie or deceive I am bound to believe it. If any other man can do differently, why, God is his judge but I believe there will be a day of reckoning.[21]

A few weeks on, Myrick responded to Camp and Robertson, calling for tolerance of different perspectives on the interpretation of these and similar stories, and for not making one approach a test of fellowship in place of faith in Christ. One paragraph gives a glimpse, a sense, of how Myrick's Spiritualism may have shaped his interactions with his fellow (more or less) Disciples:

> We both accept Christ, but for different reasons. The ground of your faith is material, of mine, spiritual and ethical. You accept Christ because he is reported to have blessed a small fish, causing it to furnish a meal for some

20. H.W.B. Myrick, "Reason and Religion," *Christian Evangelist*, March 13, 1902.
21. H.W. Robertson, "Is the Difficulty Obviated?" *Christian Evangelist*, April 10, 1902.

thousand or more hungry men, while I accept him for giving the golden rule. You believe in him because he walked on the water. I believe in him because he walked in purity and holiness. Your faith has a physical and material basis, mine rests upon a spiritual and ethical foundation.[22]

Other than being an oddly interesting figure in his own right—Stone-Campbell minister, Spiritualist lecturer, short story author, hymnist—what might the larger importance of H.W.B. Myrick be for us? I think it shows that the border between the Stone-Campbell and other religious movements was not always as clearly defined as we might assume. The Spiritualist teachings of Jesse Ferguson, of course, went beyond what the fellowship was willing to tolerate, leading to a prompt and effective reprisal from more orthodox members; but again, this was not always the case. I have written elsewhere about the SCM ties of the famous "Sleeping Prophet" Edgar Cayce, who claimed immense numbers of extraordinary visions while also serving as a deacon and teacher in Disciples' congregations around the same time as Myrick.[23] For us, then, perhaps the lesson is to not assume a uniformity of faith within a religious movement, especially one whose congregational governance and free-wheeling editorial policies gave space for the voices of those swimming well outside of the doctrinal mainstream.

22. H.W.B. Myrick, "A Reply—Myrick to his Critics," *Christian Evangelist*, May 1, 1902.

23. John Young, "Longing for a Better Country: The Stone-Campbell Movement and the Search for Atlantis," *Journal of Discipliana* 75.1 (2022), https://digitalcommons.discipleshistory.org/journalofdiscipliana/vol75/iss1/6/.

Chapter 10

"Darwin's Monkey Trot" and the Origins of Musical Parody in the Churches of Christ

POPULAR PORTRAYALS of the Scopes Monkey Trial, both then and now, have not been overly charitable to William Jennings Bryan. Bryan biographer Michael Kazin recounts how "H.L. Mencken regaled his big-city, northern readers with descriptions of Bryan's 'peculiar imbecilities' and 'theological bilge.'"[1] According to American religious historian George M. Marsden, it would only get worse. Mencken found it

> appropriate ... that Bryan had spent his last days in a 'one-horse Tennessee village,' because Bryan loved all country people, including the 'gaping primates of the upland valley,' and delighted in 'greasy victuals of the farmhouse kitchen, country smells,' and 'the tune of cocks crowing on the dunghill.'"[2]

---

1. Michael Kazin, *A Godly Hero: The Life of William Jennings* Bryan (New York: Anchor Books, 2006), 286.
2. George M. Marsden, *Fundamentalism and American Culture: The Shaping of Twentieth-Century Evangelicalism, 1870–1925* (New York: Oxford University Press, 1980), 187.

These and other harsh evaluations did much to tarnish his legacy and to discredit the Fundamentalist movement in its entirety.[3] Not all Americans were so critical, however. Many leading figures from Churches of Christ spoke highly of Bryan after his death despite differences in doctrine. Their ranks included T.B. Larimore, who, according to Earl Irvin West, claimed that "Bryan was a great and good man, a friend of the toiling millions of suffering humanity, honest, conscientious, and sincere ...."[4]

William Jennings Bryan

Bryan was also honored in song several times over. Kazin's footnotes include references to "William Jennings Bryan's Last Fight," by Vernon Dalhart, and "The Death of William Jennings Bryan," by Charlie Oaks.[5] To these can

---

3. Marsden, *Fundamentalism and American Culture*, 184.
4. Earl Irvin West, *The Search for the Ancient Order*, vol. 4 (Germantown, TN: Religious Book Service, 1987), 17.
5. Kazin, *A Godly Hero*, 299 n14–15.

be added "The John T. Scopes Trial," which was recorded separately by both Dalhart and Oaks, making Bryan-related songs something of a cottage industry for the two.[6] Still another song, though apparently never recorded for public consumption, may be the most interesting of the bunch. What else would one expect from a catchy foxtrot, with lyrics written by a Churches of Christ preacher and chaplain, lampooning Darwin's theory of evolution while also doubling as an ode to young love?

In case the tune of "Darwin's Monkey Trot" does not immediately jump to the reader's mind, some background may be in order. On July 9, 1898, John Darrell Boren was born into a large and remarkably accomplished Wynnewood, Oklahoma, family.

John Darrell Boren

<hr />

6. Recordings of all three songs, including both versions of the third, can be found at "The 1925 Scopes 'Monkey Trial,'" *History on the Net*, https://www.historyonthenet.com/authentichistory/1921-1929/4-resis tance/3-scopes/.

At the age of twenty, he married Fannie Goodwyn, and the couple quickly established a household of their own together. Though planning to enter the pharmacy business, Boren wound up representing the Churches of Christ in a debate with a Pentecostal preacher; after his strong performance, he was called on to serve as a preacher by a congregation in Big Spring, Texas, the following year. It was from Big Spring that Boren would, in 1925, set out on a fateful—and funny—road trip to Dayton, Tennessee.[7]

A full description of the events of the Scopes Monkey Trial would go well beyond the purposes of this brief chapter,[8] but a few details from Boren's recollections are worth mentioning.[9] Along with his preaching, Boren was, at the time of the trial, involved in several writing projects. He regularly contributed articles on science to a small paper, *Ribble's Ripple*, and was hoping to conclude a full-length book on science and the Bible with a section on the trial. However, money was tight, and Boren didn't feel he could afford to make the trip. Fortunately, he hit upon the idea of writing a song to pay his way, hoping that by taking the trial as his theme, he might find a sizable audience.

---

7. For the biographical material on Boren and his family in this and subsequent paragraphs, I am greatly indebted to Scott Harp for compiling materials on the preacher at "John Darrell Boren," *The Restoration Movement*, https://www.therestorationmovement.com/_states/texas/boren, jd.htm.

8. For a recent overview of the trial and its broader impact, see Brenda Wineapple, *Keeping the Faith: God, Democracy, and the Trial that Riveted a Nation* (New York: Penguin Random House, 2024).

9. Again, Scott Harp's website serves as an invaluable resource, preserving an audio recording and transcript of an interview Boren gave in 1979 on his experiences at the trial. His son, Maxie, added an introduction in 2003. Much of the information that follows comes from the interview. See "The Scopes Monkey Trial," *The Restoration Movement*, https://www.therestorationmovement.com/_states/tennessee/scopestrial.htm.

After an extended lyric-writing session, Boren tapped the local band director, Raymond Fafer, to set the words to music. Boren also hoped to convert Fafer by working with him, and to that end, he invited him along on the trip to Dayton. After setting out on the road, the two men would periodically stop, put out a sign, and sell copies of the sheet music for their tune. By the time they reached Conway, Arkansas, the pair had sold out and had to have more printed. They sold out once again in Memphis, Tennessee, and even agreed to an option with Victor Records to sell the song for $50,000. (Sadly, the song's popularity dropped off quickly after the trial, and the company did not exercise its option.)

Two versions of the lyrics to "Darwin's Monkey Trot" exist today. The first can be found in Boren's 1979 interview about his experiences at the trial; the other comes directly from the sheet music, a photocopy of which is held at the Center for Popular Music at Middle Tennessee State University.[10] I have combined the two by starting with the sheet music and adding [in brackets] the slight variations Boren gave decades later:

> Verse 1:
> *A lovely pair all dressed in hair,*
> *Darwin then said 'twas monkeys fair,*
> *But when I see a girl like you,*
> *With cheeks so red and eyes so blue,*
> *I wonder how, such things could be,*

---

10. "Darwin's Monkey Trot," Sheet Music Collection, Scopes Series, Item Number 000479-TENN. Many thanks to Ashley Armstrong for providing me with a scan.

A Jane like you with dimple knees [dim-pled
knee],
Yet, on the beach, you always tease me, About
the sights you see.

Chorus:
Billy said...
Keep up your loving boys, monkeys are dead,
Keep up your petting girls, don't lose your
    head,
Papa was a monkey in a coconut tree,
Mama was not, so don't fool around
    with me,
Just take me down to an old country lane
Or to the movies it's just the same,
Cut out the monkey stuff, tell it to Darwin
I'm just a snappy, happy little Jane.

Verse 2:
Billy said...
You are [Jane you're] my gal, just call me pal,
I love you dear, let's make a vow,
Pack up your grip, we'll take a trip,
We're [For] chimpanzees, why give a rip,
When Darrow's [Darwin's] through, with
    you and me,
We will lose our coconut tree,
And live in peace, all of our [the] years,
Down at Dayton, Tennessee.

Though it did not lead to a lasting musical career for
Boren, "Darwin's Monkey Trot" did bring him a significant
measure of fame in the short run. He was invited to sit

behind William Jennings Bryan during the trial, interviewed defense attorney Clarence Darrow, and even preached at the local Church of Christ in Dayton.

Clarence Darrow

In the years following the Dayton trip, Boren became more notable for his ministerial work. During the Great Depression, Boren brought in extra income for his family by serving as a chaplain in the Civilian Conservation Corps. His time in the CCC opened a subsequent opportunity for him to join the chaplaincy of the U.S. Army. After writing a thesis demonstrating that the Churches of Christ were in fact a distinct religious group in need of representation, Boren became the first Army chaplain from the fellowship.

Two of J.D.'s sons (Maxie and Jodie) would go on to long and distinguished preaching careers, as would his brother Dallas. Nor was J.D. the only member of his family with a real knack for music. One cousin, Helen, was a student at the Chicago Conservatory of Music; she sang (and may have recorded, though I have not found any direct evidence of it) a version of "Darwin's Monkey Trot." J.D.'s sister, Mae Boren Axton, was the co-writer of the classic "Heartbreak Hotel," helped discover and popularize Willie Nelson, and served as a PR expert for several Grand Ole Opry performers.[11] Her son, Hoyt Axton, was likewise a gifted actor and songwriter whose credits include, among many others, "Joy to the World."[12] The Boren family excelled in still other ways. Another of J.D.'s brothers, Lyle H. Boren, served as a U.S. Congressman. In turn, Lyle's son, David, was governor of Oklahoma, represented the state in the U.S. Senate, and held the presidency of its flagship university.

Today, "Weird Al" Yankovic is far and away the most famous parodist associated with the Churches of Christ, and one of its most well-known musicians and songwriters regardless of genre.

---

11. Bob Burke, "Axton, Mae Boren (1914–1997)," *Encyclopedia of Oklahoma History and Culture,* https://www.okhistory.org/publications/enc/entry?entry=AX002

12. Bob Burke, "Axton, Hoyt Wayne (1938-1999)," *Encyclopedia of Oklahoma History and Culture,* https://www.okhistory.org/publications/enc/entry?entryname=HOYT%20WAYNE%20AXTON. One side note that may be of interest is that "Joy to the World" was made famous by Three Dog Night, a band that included a member of Churches of Christ, guitarist Mike Allsup, in its lineup. See Michael W. Casey and Douglas A. Foster, "Introduction: The Renaissance of Stone-Campbell Studies," in *The Stone-Campbell Movement: An International Religious Tradition,* eds. Michael W. Casey and Douglas A. Foster (Knoxville, TN: University of Tennessee Press, 2002), 43.

"Weird Al" Yankovic

But he was not, as we have seen, the first figure from the fellowship to seek laughs through lyrics. And though "Darwin's Monkey Trot" is today little more than a footnote in the story of the Scopes Monkey Trial,[13] it remains a fascinating footnote all the same.

---

13. W. David Baird's thorough *Churches of Christ in Oklahoma* (Norman, OK: University of Oklahoma Press, 2020) does mention briefly on pages 146–147 that "In July 1925, John D. Boren, subsequently a U.S. Army chaplain and minister of a Church of Christ in Oklahoma City, attended the Scopes trial in Dayton, Tennessee, and wrote a popular song defending William Jennings Bryan."

Chapter 11

Booklets and Biographies

A Brief Historiography of Restoration Movement Resources for Young Readers

IN 1970, the preacher and historian Dabney Phillips wrote a pamphlet, *Youth and the Restoration Movement*, in which he identifies a distinct lack of interest in, and knowledge of, the movement's history among its young people. Part of the problem, he asserts early on, is the dearth of teaching resources intended for that demographic. "It is the judgment of mature Bible teachers that few of our young people have a clear conception of the restoration plea," he observes, and "There has been a scarcity of materials available for the youths of our congregations to study."[1] Across the following pages, Phillips outlines six criteria that he views as essential for any potential or future youth curricula on Restoration Movement history. They include 1) identifying the New Testament church; 2) identifying departures from that pattern; 3) clearly defining "restoration"; 4) sharing the

---

1. Dabney Phillips, *Youth and the Restoration Movement* (Tupelo, MS: Barber Printing, 1970), 3. https://digitalcommons.acu.edu/crs_books/428/. The pages of the pamphlet are unnumbered, and my pagination is based on the PDF at the link listed above.

stories of individual movement leaders; 5) communicating the importance of evangelism; and 6) demonstrating the continued relevance of the restoration plea.[2]

Phillips had the opportunity to produce a work along these lines with the 1975 publication of *Restoration Principles and Personalities*.

Dabney Phillips

Kenneth Reed, a Tuscaloosa, Alabama-area minister, shares Phillips's concerns in his introduction to the book: "Many older people are alarmed, and rightly so, because many of our Christian young people do not know anything about the Restoration Movement." Also, like Phillips, Reed places the blame not on these young people, but on older generations: "There is an obvious reason for this—we haven't taught them anything about the subject!"[3]

Since that time, relatively few writers have taken up

2.   Phillips, *Youth and the Restoration Movement*, 3–5.
3.   Kenneth Reed, "Introduction: The Relevancy of the Restoration," in

Dabney Phillips's call to action. However, there have been at least two robust efforts to communicate Restoration Movement history to younger readers. The first is a series of booklets from the Standard Publishing Company (associated with the independent Christian Churches) dating to the mid-1980s. One title, *The Church of the New Testament: One Group's Efforts to Restore the Unity of God's People*, was authored by church historian James B. North; the other four, all short biographies, were written by professor and children's book author Daniel J. Schantz.[4] (I have not been able to source a copy of the North volume, so the following observations only apply to the Schantz booklets.) The booklets are all under twenty pages, with illustrations and sidebars to break up the main text. All four place emphasis on the childhood and young adult years of the restorers being profiled—Alexander Campbell, Walter Scott, Raccoon John Smith, and Barton W. Stone—and kid-friendly tidbits like Scott's knack for interacting with children receive special attention.[5]

Dabney Phillips, *Restoration Principles and Personalities* (University, AL: Youth in Action, Inc., 1975), 10.

4. These include, all by Daniel Schantz, *Alexander Campbell: Restoration Nobleman* (Cincinnati, OH: Standard Publishing Company, 1984); *Barton W. Stone: A Bright Star* (Cincinnati, OH: Standard Publishing Company, 1984; *Raccoon John Smith: Homespun Preacher* (Cincinnati, OH: Standard Publishing Company, 1984); and *Walter Scott: God's Pied Piper* (Cincinnati, OH: Standard Publishing Company, 1984).

5. Schantz, *Walter Scott*, 12.

Walter Scott

"Raccoon" John Smith

The lessons also draw connections to outside historical

references, such as various goings-on in American history and the novelists Mark Twain and Sir Walter Scott.[6]

The other substantive effort to communicate Restoration Movement history to young readers (of which I am aware, at least) came five years later with the publication of Carol Brown's *The Disciple from Bethany: The Adventures of Alexander Campbell* by Abilene Christian University Press. This book is considerably longer than Schantz's booklets but is still aimed at younger readers; it shares with the earlier works a clear biographical focus and an interest in the early life of its protagonist. From the first page of the book, Brown offers relatable anecdotes to try to get audience members to identify with Campbell, even if they have little interest in movement history: "'Alexander! Wake up! That cow has more French in her stomach than you have in your head,' Thomas Campbell scolded his nine-year-old son sleeping under a tree on a warm summer afternoon."[7]

The foreword to the book is provided by Brown's friend, the noted Restoration Movement historian Bill Humble. Humble shares many of the same perspectives as Brown, as well as Phillips and Reed above:

> It must have been at least three years ago that Carol Brown came by my home for a visit. Carol said, "I'm afraid that young people growing up in our churches today don't know anything about our restoration heritage. They haven't heard about men like Barton Stone and Alexander Campbell and how much we owe to them. So I

---

6. Schantz, *Alexander Campbell*, 3; Schantz, *Barton W. Stone*, 14; Schantz, *Walter Scott*, 3.

7. Carol Brown, *The Disciple from Bethany: The Adventures of Alexander Campbell* (Abilene, TX: ACU Press, 1989), 1.

have been thinking about writing a book for young people about Alexander Campbell's life" ... Carol is right. The young people in our churches cannot think of early restoration leaders as "heroes of the faith" for the simple reason they haven't heard of them.[8]

Without disparaging the efforts of the authors and publishers of these resources, Sunday School teachers would likely have a hard time building a class around any or all of them. For one, the materials are all somewhat dated in terms of their presentation and references; students would likely still understand a mention of Mark Twain, but Walter Scott (the writer, not the restorer) would probably be a bridge too far. Of course, older materials can still be quite helpful if they can be acquired cheaply and/or easily; however, neither is the case here. I have already noted above my inability to locate an accessible copy of the North pamphlet. Of the four Schantz booklets, I managed to find used copies of two online; both were pricy, and one turned out to be a bootlegged copy. A third was available to check out from the Internet Archive, and I had to make a trip to a local Christian university library to see and use their copy of the fourth. The Carol Brown biography of Alexander Campbell was a serendipitously inexpensive find for me at a used bookstore a few years ago; at the time of this writing, there are a few copies available for purchase online, but they all run in the $15–20 range, making it costly to source for anything more than the smallest of classes.

The other major concern is that, with the seeming exception of the North pamphlet, all the works are primarily or exclusively biographical in scope. Phillips's

---

8. Bill Humble, foreword, in Brown, *The Disciple from Bethany*, ix.

book does offer some broader reflections on the history and meaning of "restoration," but even there, the balance leans heavily toward biography. This is understandable given the need to hold readers' attention with relatable anecdotes, but at the same time, more work would be needed to help students integrate the various stories into a more cohesive whole.

Still, there is much in these works to praise. If one adopts Phillips's criteria for the moment, the resources from the 1980s are especially successful in achieving goals 4–6, and Phillips's own book (unsurprisingly) scores highly across the board. And even if one defines success differently, these materials could be a valuable jumping-off point for further work and an inspiration to someone seeking to train young readers in the way they should go.

Bibliography

"The 1925 Scopes 'Monkey Trial,'" *History on the Net*, https://www.historyonthenet.com/authentichistory/1921-1929/4-resistance/3-scopes/.

"Abraham Lincoln and Tennessee." *The Lehrman Institute Presents: Abraham Lincoln's Classroom*. https://www.abrahamlincolnsclassroom.org/abraham-lincoln-state-by-state/abraham-lincoln-and-tennessee.

Alvarez, Carmelo. "The Stone-Campbell Movement in Latin America and the Caribbean," *Leaven* 17.3 (2009): 125.

Anderson, Delonda. "Hidden Scandal: a Woman, a Gun, and a President." *Appalachia Bare*, August 17, 2021. https://www.appalachiabare.com/hidden-scandal-a-woman-a-gun-and-a-president/.

Archer, Tim. "What Can't Be Embargoed: US-Cuban Church Relations." *Missio Dei Journal* 14 (2023). https://missiodeijournal.com/issues/md-14/authors/md-14-archer.

Babbitt, Colton. "Caudill Under El Caudillo: Southern Baptists, Cuba, and the Origins of Conservatism, 1959–1979. MA thesis, Florida Atlantic University, 2019.

Bacon, Cheryl Mann. "Members of House, Senate have ties to Churches of Christ." *Christian Chronicle*, January 18, 2021. https://christianchronicle.org/members-of-house-senate-have-ties-to-churches-of-christ/.

Baird, W. David. *Churches of Christ in Oklahoma*. Norman, OK: University of Oklahoma Press, 2020.

Barstow, Daniel, and Lowell Bergman. "A Family's Fortune, a Legacy of Blood and Tears." *New York Times*, January 9, 2003.

"Bibliografia," https://juanantoniomonroy.eicpos.com/bibliografia-2/.

Bitran, Tara, and Phillipe Thao. "Everything to Know About Benioff and Weiss' *Death by Lightning*." https://www.netflix.com/tudum/articles/death-by-lightning-tv-series-adaptation.

Blechman, Andrew D. *Leisureville: Adventures in a World Without Children*. New York: Grove Press, 2008.

Bond, James E. *I Dissent: The Legacy of Chief Justice James Clark McReynolds*. Fairfax, VA: George Mason University Press, 1992.

Brown, Carol. *The Disciple from Bethany: The Adventures of Alexander Campbell*. Abilene, TX: ACU Press, 1989.

Burke, Bob, "Axton, Hoyt Wayne (1938–1999)." *Encyclopedia of Oklahoma History and Culture*. https://www.okhistory.org/publications/enc/entry?entryname=HOYT%20WAYNE%20AXTON.

———. "Axton, Mae Boren (1914–1997)." *Encyclopedia of Oklahoma History and Culture*. https://www.okhistory.org/publications/enc/entry?entry=AX002.

Burns, Harliana. "From Sworn Enemies to Nazi Neighbors to Found Family: The Impact of a World War II German POW Camp on a Rural Tennessee Community and the POWs Who Lived There." MA thesis, Middle Tennessee State University, 2021.

"C. Phillip McWane." Alabama Business Hall of Fame. https://abhof.culverhouse.ua.edu/member/c-phillip-mcwane/.

Camp, Geo. T. "Reply to HWB Myrick." *Christian Evangelist*. April 3, 1902.

Cantrell, Gregg. "Lyndon's Granddaddy: Samuel Ealy Johnson Sr., Texas Populism, and the Improbable Roots of American Liberalism." *Southwestern Historical Quarterly* 118.2 (October 2014): 132–156.

Carnegie, Andrew. "The Gospel of Wealth." 6. https://media.carnegie.org/filer_public/ab/c9/abc9fb4b-dc86-4ce8-ae31-a983b9a326ed/ccny_essay_1889_thegospelofwealth.pdf.

Casey, Michael W. "From Religious Outsiders to Insiders: The Rise and Fall of Pacifism in the Churches of Christ." *Journal of Church and State* 44.3 (Summer 2002): 464 n47.

Casey, Michael W., and Douglas A. Foster. "Introduction: The Renaissance of Stone-Campbell Studies," Page 43 in *The Stone-Campbell Movement: An International Religious Tradition*. Edited by Michael W. Casey and Douglas A. Foster. Knoxville, TN: University of Tennessee Press, 2002.

Casey, Michael W., and Douglas A. Foster, eds., *The Stone-Campbell Movement: An International Religious Tradition*. Knoxville, TN: University of Tennessee Press, 2002.

Clayton, Lawrence A., and Michael L. Conniff. *A History of Modern Latin America*. 2nd ed. Belmont, CA: Thomson Wadsworth, 2005.

Coates, Neal, and Sean Evans. "The Political Awakening: Members of the Church of Christ in Congress." Paper presented at Christian Scholars' Conference, Lubbock, TX, June 2019.

"Commencement Exercises at Berry School to Begin April 29 and Close May 2," *Rome Tribune-Herald*, April 20, 1916.

Compton, John W. *The Evangelical Origins of the Living Constitution*. Cambridge, MA: Harvard University Press, 2014.

Cooper, Derek. *Introduction to World Christian History*. Downers Grove, IL: IVP Academic, 2016.

Cotten, Christopher R. "'A Relentless Warfare Against the Inventions and Devices of Man': John T. Lewis and the Churches of Christ in Birmingham, Alabama, 1907–1967." MDiv thesis, Lipscomb University, 2013.

Crawford, Wes. "Churches of Christ and Lost Cause Religion: One Southern Denomination's Attempt to Find Identity in Post-Civil War America," *Restoration Quarterly* 64.1 (2022): 11.

Cross, Randy K. "Introduction" in T.S. Stribling, *The Forge: An Epic Novel of the War-Torn South*. New York: Doubleday, Doran & Company, 1931; Tuscaloosa, AL: University of Alabama Press, 1985.

Cubstead, Lane. "History as the Firm Foundation Made It." *Firm Foundation* (April 28, 1959): 259.

Cunningham, O. Edward. *Shiloh and the Western Campaign of 1862*. Edited by Gary D. Joiner and Timothy B. Smith. New York: Savas Beatie, 2007.

Dalke, Anne French. "'Love ought to be like religion, Brother Milt': An Examination of the Civil War and Reconstruction Trilogy of T.S. Stribling." *Southern Literary Journal* 14.1 (Fall 1981): 29–30.

"Darwin's Monkey Trot." Sheet Music Collection. Scopes Series. Item Number 000479-TENN.

Dormady, Jason H. *Primitive Revolution: Restorationist Religion and the Idea of the Mexican Revolution, 1940–1968*. Albuquerque, NM: University of New Mexico Press, 2011.

Dyleski, Kate G. "First Christian Church, Sunday Morning Worship: All Are Welcome as God Has Welcomed Us." *Magic City Religion: Observations on Religion in Birmingham, Alabama, by Samford University Religious Studies Students*, May 20, 2021. https://magiccityreligion. org/2021/05/20/first-christian-church-birmingham-disciples-of-christ-sunday-morning-worship/.

Fea, John. *Believe Me: The Evangelical Road to Donald Trump*. Grand Rapids, MI: Eerdmans, 2018.

Fehrman, Craig. *Author in Chief: The Untold Story of Our Presidents and the Books They Wrote*. New York: Avid Reader Press, 2020.

Fehrman, Craig, ed. *The Best Presidential Writing from 1789 to the Present*. New York: Avid Reader Press, 2020.

Fernandez, Jose Antonio., and Timothy Archer. *A History of Churches of Christ in Cuba*. Abilene, TX: Herald of Truth Publications, 2015.

Fertig, Walter L. "Maurice Thompson's Primitive Baptist Heritage," *Indiana Magazine of History* 64.1 (March 1968): 7.

Fikes, Jason. "Jesse P. Sewell, White Supremacy, and the Formative Years of Abilene Christian College," *Restoration Quarterly* 64.3 (2022): 176.

"First Christian Church." Bhamwiki. https://www.bhamwiki.com/w/First_Christian_Church.

Foster, Douglas A. "Larimore, Theophilus Brown (1843–1929)." Pages 452–453 in *The Encyclopedia of the Stone-Campbell Movement.* Edited by Douglas A. Foster, Paul M. Blowers, Anthony L. Dunnavant, and D. Newell Williams. Grand Rapids, MI: Eerdmans, 2004.

Freyer, Tony. *Hugo L. Black and the Dilemma of American Liberalism.* Glenview, IL: Scott, Foresman/Little, Brown Higher Education, 1990.

Gardner, Terry. "Austin McGary." *The Restoration Movement.* https://www.therestorationmovement.com/_states/texas/mcgary,austin.htm.

Gardner, Terry J. "McGary, Austin (1846-1928)," Pages 507–508 in *The Encyclopedia of the Stone-Campbell Movement.* Edited by Douglas A. Foster, Paul M. Blowers, Anthony L. Dunnavant, and D. Newell Williams. Grand Rapids, MI: Eerdmans, 2004.

"Gentry County's Oldest Preacher Dies: Henry Ward Beecher Myrick, of Gentryville, Succumbs—Had a Varied Career." *King City Chronicle.* February 18, 1937.

Goodyear, C.W. *President Garfield: From Radical to Unifier.* New York: Simon & Schuster, 2023.

Grant, Carl A., and Shelby J. Grant. *The Moment: Barack Obama, Jeremiah Wright, and the Firestorm at Trinity United Church of Christ.* Lanham, MD: Rowman & Littlefield Publishers, 2013.

Guthrie, John J., Jr. "Seeking the Sweet Spirit of Harmony: Establishing a Spiritualist Community at Cassadaga, Florida, 1893-1933." *Florida Historical Quarterly* 77.1 (1998): 1–38.

Haley, T.P. *Early Missouri Preachers.* 2 vols. St. Louis, MO: Christian Publishing Co., 1888; repr. ed. Henderson, TN: Hester Publications.

Harlow, A. F. "James R. McWane: Who finds it profitable to study his equipment and to study his men." *System,* November 1920.

Harp, Scott, compiler. "John Darrell Boren." *The Restoration Movement,* https://www.therestorationmovement.com/_states/texas/boren,jd.htm

———. "The Scopes Monkey Trial." *The Restoration Movement.* https://www.therestorationmovement.com/_states/tennessee/scopestrial.htm.

Hatch, Nathan O. *The Democratization of American Christianity.* New Haven, CT: Yale University Press, 1989.

Hicks, Jacob. "The Legend of George Washington's Baptism." *Digital Encyclopedia of George Washington.* https://www.mountvernon.org/

library/digitalhistory/digital-encyclopedia/article/the-legend-of-george-washington-s-baptism.

"History." United Church of Christ. https://www.ucc.org/who-we-are/about/history/.

Holcombe, William O., Claradel Holcombe, and Jimmy Langley. *First Christian Church Birmingham: 150 Years: A History* (2024).

Holton, A. R. "75 Years Advancing With Texas." *Firm Foundation.* (January 20, 1959): 38.

Hopen, David. *The Orchard: A Novel.* New York: HarperCollins, 2020.

Hughes, Richard T., and James L. Gorman. *Reviving the Ancient Faith: The Story of Churches of Christ in America.* 3rd ed. Grand Rapids, MI: Eerdmans, 2024.

Humble, Bill. "Foreword." Page ix in *The Disciple from Bethany: The Adventures of Alexander Campbell.* Carol Brown. Abilene, TX: ACU Press, 1989.

"James Henry Stribling, 1863–1951." https://www.therestorationmovement.com/_states/tennessee/stribling.htm.

Johnson, Nicholas. *Big Dead Place: Inside the Strange and Menacing World of Antarctica,* Los Angeles: Feral House, 2005.

Jones, John M., and Michael W. Casey. "Ronald Reagan, the Disciples of Christ, and Restoring America." Pages 196–212 in *And the WORD Became Flesh: Studies in History, Communication, and Scripture in Memory of Michael W. Casey.* Edited by Thomas H. Olbricht and David Fleer. Eugene, OR: Pickwick Publications, 2009.

Kazin, Michael. *A Godly Hero: The Life of William Jennings Bryan.* New York: Anchor Books, 2006.

Kennedy, David M. *Freedom from Fear: The American People in Depression and War, 1929–1945.* New York: Oxford University Press, 1999.

Kimbrough, Earl. *The Warrior from Rock Creek: Life, Times, and Thoughts of F.B. Srygley, 1859–1940.* Louisville, KY: Religious Supply Center, 2008.

Kirkland, Scotty. "Retrospect: ACIPCO President John J. Eagan applied 'Golden Rule' to industry." *Business Alabama,* September 28, 2023. https://businessalabama.com/retrospect-acipco-president-john-j-eagan-applies-golden-rule-to-industry/.

Konigsburg, E.L. *The View from Saturday.* New York: Scholastic, 1996.

LaFantasie, Glenn W. "The Mystery of Lincoln's Second Flatboat Trip to New Orleans." *Friends of the Lincoln Collection.* https://www.friendsofthelincolncollection.org/lincoln-lore/the-mystery-of-lincolns-second-flatboat-trip-to-new-orleans/.

Lamar, Clarinda Pendleton. *The Life of Joseph Rucker Lamar, 1857–1916.*

New York: G.P. Putnam's Sons, 1926.

Larimore, Emma Page. *Life, Letters, and Sermons of T.B. Larimore*. Nashville, TN: Gospel Advocate, 1931.

———. *Letters and Sermons of T.B. Larimore*. Vol. 3. McQuiddy Printing Company, 1910.

———. *Our Corner Book: From Maine to Mexico, From Canada to Cuba*. Nashville, TN: Publishing House of the M.E. Church, South, 1912.

Lozada, Carlos. *What Were We Thinking: A Brief Intellectual History of the Trump Era*. New York: Simon & Schuster, 2020.

McClintock, James *Lost Antarctica: Adventures in a Disappearing Land*. New York: St. Martin's Griffin, 2012.

McDonald, Forrest. *The American Presidency: An Intellectual History*. Lawrence, KS: University Press of Kansas, 1994.

McPherson, James M. *Battle Cry of Freedom: The Civil War Era*. New York: Oxford University Press, 1988.

McWane, J.R. "Standard Lengths of Cast Iron Pipe Cast Horizontally." *Journal AWWA* 16.5 (November 1926): 620–624.

Marsden, George M. *Fundamentalism and American Culture: The Shaping of Twentieth-Century Evangelicalism, 1870–1925*. New York: Oxford University Press, 1980.

Martin, Jim. "The Secret Baptism of Abraham Lincoln," *Restoration Quarterly* 38.2 (1996): 65–76.

Materials from *Clinton Advertiser*. August 4, 1920. https://iagenweb.org/clinton/places/clinton/spiritualist.html.

"Message on the 25th Anniversary of the Antarctic Treaty." November 26, 1984. https://www.reaganlibrary.gov/archives/speech/message-25th-anniversary-antarctic-treaty.

Monroy, Juan Antonio. *An Autobiography*. Translated by Carolina Tolosa Archer. Abilene, TX: ACU Press, 2011.

Moorhouse, William Mervin. "The Restoration Movement: The Rhetoric of Jacksonian Restorationism in a Frontier Religion." PhD diss., Indiana University, 1967.

Mosely, J. Edward. *Disciples of Christ in Georgia*. St. Louis, MO: The Bethany Press, 1954.

Myrick, H.W.B. "The Bachelors' Club." *New York Weekly*. May 25, 1885. https://dimenovels.org/Item/65732/Show.

———. "Fore-knowledge." *Christian Quarterly Review*. April 1883.

———. "Inspiration." *Christian Quarterly Review*. October 1882.

———. "James J. Evans Died Saturday: Death Claimed Well Known Gentry County Farmer at His Home Near Here Last Saturday

Night." *Stanberry Headlight*. September 2, 1937. https://web.
pdx.edu/~davide/gene/Evans_James_Johnson.htm.

———. "Martin Miller Called by Death: Local Resident Dies At Home
After Illness of Asthma and Heart Disease." *Shelbyville Republican*.
July 25, 1933. https://www.shelbycountyindiana.org/obituaries/
obit_miller.htm.

———. "Obituary for Martha Jane Sampson Yeater." *Ledger*. June 22,
1906, https://www.findagrave.com/memorial/18236538/martha_
jane-yeater.

———. "A Peculiar People." *National Spiritualist*. September 1978.

——— "Reason and Religion." *Christian Evangelist*. March 13, 1902.

———. "A Reply—Myrick to his Critics." *Christian Evangelist*. May 1,
1902.

———. "What a Set of Whiskers Did." *New York Weekly*. October 31,
1881. https://dimenovels.org/Item/85407/Show.

"News Items of Interest." *Florence Times*. November 13, 1908.

"The Normal College—Interesting Commencement Exercises." *Florence
Times*. June 5, 1903.

Nottingham, William J., and William J. Morgan. "Latin America and the
Caribbean, Missions in, 1. Christian Church (Disciples of Christ),"
Page 457 in *Encyclopedia of the Stone-Campbell Movement*. Edited by
Douglas A. Foster, Paul M. Blowers, Anthony L. Dunnavant, and D.
Newell Williams. Grand Rapids, MI: Eerdmans, 2004.

Obama, Barack. *A Promised Land*. New York: Crown, 2020.

Peppers, Todd C. "Cancelling Justice? The Case of James Clark
McReynolds." *Richmond Public Interest Law Review* 24.2 (2021): 68–
69.

Phillips, Dabney. *Youth and the Restoration Movement*. Tupelo, MS:
Barber Printing, 1970. https://digitalcommons.acu.edu/crs_
books/428/.

"Plans for Y.M.C.A. Building Underway," *Dubuque Telegraph-Herald*,
April 11, 1915.

"President's Memorandum Regarding Antarctica." February 5, 1982.
https://www.nsf.gov/geo/opp/ant/memo_6646.jsp.

Pruden, William. "Joseph Rucker Lamar." *New Georgia Encyclopedia*.
https://www.georgiaencyclopedia.org/articles/government-politics/
joseph-rucker-lamar-1857-1916/.

Reed, Kenneth. "Introduction: The Relevancy of the Restoration." Page 10
in Dabney Phillips, *Restoration Principles and Personalities*. University, AL: Youth in Action, 1975.

Richey, Frank. *Vignettes of Virtue: Short Stories of the American Restoration Movement*. Florence, AL: Cypress Creek Book Company, 2010.

Robertson, H.W. "Is the Difficulty Obviated?" *Christian Evangelist*. April 10, 1902.

Ross, Bobby, Jr., "For Cuba, a Time of Stress—and Salvation" *Christian Chronicle*, November 14, 2023. https://christianchronicle.org/for-cuba-a-time-of-stress-and-salvation/.

Rushford, Jerry Bryant. "'The Apollos of the West': The Life of John Allen Gano." MA thesis, Abilene Christian College, 1972.

———. "Political Disciple: The Relationship Between James A. Garfield and the Disciples of Christ." PhD diss., University of California Santa Barbara, 1977. https://digitalcommons.pepperdine.edu/heritage_center/7/.

Schantz, Daniel. *Alexander Campbell: Restoration Nobleman*. Cincinnati, OH: Standard Publishing Company, 1984.

———. *Barton W. Stone: A Bright Star*. Cincinnati, OH: Standard Publishing Company, 1984.

———. *Raccoon John Smith: Homespun Preacher*. Cincinnati, OH: Standard Publishing Company, 1984.

———. *Walter Scott: God's Pied Piper*. Cincinnati, OH: Standard Publishing Company, 1984.

Scheb, John M., II. "McReynolds, James Clark." Page 629 in *The Oxford Companion to the Supreme Court of the United States*. Edited by James W. Ely and Joel B. Grossman. New York: Oxford University Press, 2005.

Scott, Ronald W. "Protecting United States Interests in Antarctica." *San Diego Law Review* 26 (1989): 575–623.

Sensing, Tim. "Lamar, James Sanford (1829-1908)." Pages 449–450 in *The Encyclopedia of the Stone-Campbell Movement*. Edited by Douglas A. Foster, Paul M. Blowers, Anthony L. Dunnavant, and D. Newell Williams. Grand Rapids, MI: Eerdmans, 2004.

Smith, Gary Scott. *Faith and the Presidency; From George Washington to George W. Bush*. New York: Oxford University Press, 2006.

Smith, Timothy B. *Rethinking Shiloh: Myth and Memory*. Knoxville, TN: University of Tennessee Press, 2013.

Some Kind of Heaven. directed by Lance Oppenheim, produced by Darren Aronofsky. 2020; Magnolia Pictures, 2021. Prime Video. https://www.amazon.com/gp/video/detail/B08SQ9W7VR/ref=msx_wn_av.

Spurlock, Jefferson T. "T.S. Stribling." *Encyclopedia of Alabama*. https://encyclopediaofalabama.org/article/t-s-stribling/.

Srygley, F. D. *Biographies and Sermons: A Collection of Original Sermons by Different Men, with a Biographical Sketch of Each Man Accompanying His Sermon, Illustrated by Half-Tone Cuts.* Nashville, TN: Gospel Advocate Company, 1961.

———. *Smiles and Tears: Or, Larimore and His Boys.* n.d.: F. D. Srygley, 1889.

Stanback, C. Foster. *Into All Nations: A History of the International Churches of Christ.* Newton Upper Falls, MA: Illumination Publishers International, 2005.

"Statement on Signing the Montreal Protocol on Ozone-Depleting Substances." April 5, 1988. https://www.reaganlibrary.gov/archives/speech/statement-signing-montreal-protocol-ozone-depleting-substances.

Steenson, Ashley. "A War of Ideas: L.Q.C. Lamar and American Political Thought." MA thesis, University of Mississippi, 2020.

"A Stone-Campbell 'Father' on the Ku Klux Klan," https://johnmarkhicks.com/2011/12/31/a-stone-campbell-father-on-the-ku-klux-klan/.

Stribling, T.S. *Laughing Stock: The Posthumous Autobiography.* Edited by Randy K. Cross and John T. McMillan. Memphis, TN: St. Luke's Press, 1982.

———. "Persia Hiram Hooten." *Gospel Advocate.* August 3, 1905.

———. *The Store: A Stirring Novel of the Post-Reconstruction South* (New York: Doubleday, Doran & Company, 1932; Tuscaloosa, AL: University of Alabama Press, 1985.

"There remaineth a rest." *Hymnary.* https://hymnary.org/text/far_down_the_misty_aisle.

"Two Companies, Two Visions." *Frontline.* https://www.pbs.org/wgbh/pages/frontline/shows/workplace/mcwane/two.html.

Varon, Elizabeth R. "Andrew Johnson: Life Before the Presidency." *UVA Miller Center.* https://millercenter.org/president/johnson/life-before-the-presidency.

Vickers, Kenneth W. *T.S. Stribling: A Life of the Tennessee Novelist.* Knoxville, TN: University of Tennessee Press, 2004.

Walker, Philip A., Jr. "Lyndon B. Johnson's Senate Foreign Policy Activism: The Suez Canal Crisis, a Reappraisal." *Presidential Studies Quarterly* 26.4 (Fall 1996): 99–1008.

Watson, George H., and Mildred B. Watson. *History of the Christian Churches in the Alabama Area.* St. Louis: The Bethany Press, 1965.

West, Earl Irvin. *The Search for the Ancient Order: A History of the Restoration Movement.* Vol. 2, 1866–1906. Indianapolis: Religious Book Service, 1950.

———. *The Search for the Ancient Order: A History of the Restoration Movement.* Vol. 3, 1900-1918. Indianapolis: Religious Book Service, 1979.

———*The Search for the Ancient Order.* Vol. 4. Germantown, TN: Religious Book Service, 1987.

"William McWane," Alabama Business Hall of Fame. https://abhof.culver house.ua.edu/member/william-mcwane/.

Williams, D. Newell, Douglas A. Foster, and Paul M. Blowers, eds. *The Stone-Campbell Movement: A Global History.* St. Louis, MO: Chalice Press, 2013.

Wilson, Eric G. *The Spiritual History of Ice: Romanticism, Science, and the Imagination.* New York: Palgrave Macmillan, 2003.

Wineapple, Brenda. *Keeping the Faith: God, Democracy, and the Trial that Riveted a Nation.* New York: Penguin Random House, 2024.

Winkle, John W., III. "Lamar, Joseph Rucker." Page 569 in *The Oxford Companion to the Supreme Court of the United States.* Edited by James W. Ely and Joel B. Grossman. New York: Oxford University Press, 2005.

Wynne, Nick, and Joe Knetsch. *Utopian Communities of Florida: A History of Hope.* Charleston, SC: The History Press, 2016.

Young, Ed. "James Clark McReynolds." *Tennessee Encyclopedia.* https://tennesseeencyclopedia.net/entries/james-clark-mcreynolds/.

Young, John. "Disciples of Christ and The University of Alabama School of Religion That Wasn't." *Alabama Review* 75.3 (July 2022): 199–224.

———. "Dixieland's Demise: T.B. Larimore's Dixieland College and the Tenuous Position of Christian Colleges within the Churches of Christ." *Restoration Quarterly* 58,.3 (2016): 143–159.

———. "The House of 'Mirrors': A Historical-Statistical Analysis of Five Lectureships Associated with Churches of Christ-Affiliated Schools, 1920–2020." *Restoration Quarterly* 65.3 (2023): 171–179.

———. "Longing for a Better Country: The Stone-Campbell Movement and the Search for Atlantis." *Journal of Discipliana* 75.1 (2022)

———. *Redrawing the Blueprints for the Early Church: Historical Ecclesiology in and around the Stone-Campbell Movement.* Florence, AL: Heritage Christian University Press, 2021.

———. *Visions of Restoration: The History of Churches of Christ.* Florence, AL: Cypress Publications, 2019.

About the Author

John Young is an associate professor in the Turner School of Theology at Amridge University and an adjunct instructor in the Bible Department at Mars Hill Bible School. His previous publications with Heritage Christian University Press/Cypress Publications include *Visions of Restoration: The History of Churches of Christ* (2019); *Redrawing the Blueprints for the Early Church: Historical Ecclesiology in and around the Stone-Campbell Movement* (2021); and, as coeditor with Rickey Collum, *Near to the Brokenhearted: Funeral Sermon Outlines* (2024).

Also by John Young

Rickey Collum and John Young, editors, *Near to the Brokenhearted: Funeral Sermon Outlines*. Florence, AL: Cypress Publications, 2024.

Redrawing the Blueprints for the Early Church: Historical Ecclesiology in and around the Stone-Campbell Movement. Florence, AL: Heritage Christian University Press, 2021.

Visions of Restoration: The History of Churches of Christ. Florence, AL: Cypress Publications, 2019.

CYPRESS
PUBLICATIONS
An Imprint of Heritage Christian University Press

To see full catalog of Heritage Christian University Press
and its imprint Cypress Publications, visit
www.hcu.edu/publications